Workbook 2

Managing Yourself

Manage People
Certificate
S/NVQ Level 4

Institute of Management Open Learning Programme

Series editor: Gareth Lewis
Author: Lisa Davis

the Institute of Management

Pergamon
Flexible
Learning

Pergamon Open Learning
An imprint of Butterworth-Heinemann
Linacre House, Jordan Hill, Oxford OX2 8DP
225 Wildwood Avenue, Woburn, MA 01801-2041
A division of Reed Educational and Professional Publishing Ltd

R A member of the Reed Elsevier plc group

OXFORD   AUCKLAND   BOSTON
JOHANNESBURG   MELBOURNE   NEW DELHI

First published 1997
Reprinted 1998, 1999, 2000

British Library Cataloguing in Publication Data
A catalogue record for this book is available from the British Library

ISBN 0 7506 3661 0

Typeset by Avocet Typeset, Brill, Aylesbury, Bucks
Printed and bound in Great Britain

Contents

Series overview

The Institute of Management Open Learning Programme is a series of workbooks prepared by the Institute of Management and Pergamon Open Learning for managers seeking to develop themselves.

Comprising seventeen open learning workbooks, the programme covers the best of modern management theory and practice, and each workbook provides a range of frameworks and techniques to improve your effectiveness as a manager, thus helping you acquire the knowledge and skill to make you fully competent in your role.

Each workbook is written by an experienced management writer and covers an important management topic or theme. The activities both reinforce learning and help to relate the generic ideas to your individual work context. While coverage of each topic is fully comprehensive, additional reading suggestions and reference sources are given for those who wish to study to a greater depth.

Designed to be practical, stimulating and challenging, the aim of the workbooks is to improve performance at work by benefiting you and your organization. This practical focus is at the heart of the competence based approach that has been adopted by the programme.

The structure of the programme

The design and overall structure of the programme has two main organizing principles, both of which are closely linked to the national standards for management developed by the MCI (Management Charter Initiative).

First, the workbooks are grouped according to the key roles of management.

- Underpinning the management standards are a series of **personal competences** which describe the personal skills required by all managers, which are essential to skill in all the main functional or key role areas.
- **Manage Activities** describes the principles of managing processes and activities, with service to the customer as an essential part of this.
- **Manage Resources** describes the acquisition, control and monitoring of financial and other resources.
- **Manage People** looks at the key skills involved in leadership, developing one's staff and managing their performance.

- **Manage Information** discusses the acquisition, storage and use of information for communication, problem solving and decision making.

In addition, there are three specialized key roles: **Manage Quality, Manage Projects** and **Manage Energy**. The workbooks cover the first two of these. Unlike the four primary key roles above, these are not compulsory for certificate, diploma or S/NVQ requirements, but provide options for the latter.

Together, these key roles provide a comprehensive description of the fundamental principles of management as it applies in any organization – commercial, maintained sector or not-for-profit.

Second, the programme is organized according to **levels of management**, seniority and responsibility.

Level 4 represents first line management. In accredited programmes this is equivalent to S/NVQ Level 4, Certificate in Management or CMS. Level 5 is equivalent to middle/senior management and is accredited at S/NVQ Level 5, Diploma in Management or DMS. There are two S/NVQs at Level 5: Operational Management and Strategic Management. The operations role is focussed internally within an organization on the maintenance of systems and standards of output, whilst the strategic role is focussed on the whole organization, including the external operating environment, and looks at setting directions.

Together, the workbooks cover all the background knowledge you need to have for all units of competence in the MCI standards at Level 4 and Level 5 (apart from the specialized units in the key role Manage Energy). They also provide skills development and opportunities for portfolio building.

For a comprehensive list of workbooks, see page ix. For a comprehensive list of links with the standards, see the *User Guide*.

How to use the programme

The programme is deliberately designed to be flexible and can be used in a variety of ways:

- to update on important management topics and themes, or develop individual skills: as the workbooks are grouped according to themes, it should be easy for you to pick out one that suits your needs

- as part of generic management development programmes: you can choose the modules that fit the themes of the programme

■ as part of, and in support of, accredited competence-based programmes.

For N/SVQs at both Levels 4 and 5, there are options in the combinations of units that make up the various awards. By using the map provided in the *User Guide*, individuals will be able to select the workbooks appropriate to their specific needs, and their chosen accreditation options. Some of the activities will help you provide evidence for your portfolio; where we think this is the case, we give the relevant reference to the standards.

For Certificate or CMS, Diploma or DMS, individuals should choose modules that not only meet their individual needs but also satisfy the requirements of the delivering body and the awarding body.

You may need help and guidance in these choices, and the *User Guide* sets out the options and advice in much more detail. A fuller description of the potential uses of this material in evidence gathering and portfolio building can also be found in the *User Guide*, as can a detailed description of the contents of each workbook.

Workbooks in the Institute of Management Open Learning Programme

Manage People (Level 5)

14 *The New Model Leader*

Manage Information (Level 4)

15 *Making Rational Decisions*
16 *Communication*

Manage Information (Level 5)

17 *Successful Information Management*

Manage Quality (Level 4)

3 *Understanding Business Process Management**
4 *Customer Focus**

Manage Quality (Level 5)

5 *Getting TQM to Work**

Manage Projects (Level 4)

8 *Project Management**

Manage Projects (Level 5)

8 *Project Management**

Support Materials

18 *User Guide*
19 *Mentor Guide*

An asterisk indicates that a particular workbook also contains material suitable for a particular key role or personal competence over and above that where it is principally designated.

Links to qualifications

S/NVQ programmes

This workbook can help candidates to achieve credit and develop skills in the key role Manage People at Level 4, and covers the following units and elements:

C5   Develop productive working relationships
C5.1 Develop the trust and support of colleagues and team members
C5.2 Develop the trust and support of your manager
C5.3 Minimize interpersonal conflict
C6   Enhance productive working relationships
C6.1 Enhance the trust and support of colleagues
C6.2 Enhance the trust and support of those to whom you report

It is also relevant to some of the personal competences.

Certificate and Diploma programmes

This workbook, together with the other workbooks on managing people (1 – *The Influential Manager,* 11 – *Getting the Right People to do the Right Job*, 12 – *Developing Yourself and Your Staff*, 13 – *Building a High Performance Team* and 14 – *The New Model Leader*), covers all of the knowledge required in the key role Manage People for Certificate in Management and CMS programmes as well as Diploma in Management and DMS programmes.

Links to other workbooks

Other workbooks in the key role Manage People (at Level 4) are:

1 *The Influential Manager*

11 *Getting the Right People to do the Right Job*

12 *Developing Yourself and Your Staff*

13 *Building a High Performance Team*

And at Level 5:

14 *The New Model Leader*

The theme of this workbook is closely associated with:

16 *Communication*

Introduction

When people talk about 'the role of the manager' the focus is usually external and looks outwards from the person who is doing the managing. So there is much talk of managing resources, people, tasks and processes.

But efficient and effective management really begins 'at home'. In much the same way as we expect doctors to manage their own health – *'physician, heal thyself'* – most organizations expect their managers to be good at managing themselves. The thinking goes that if someone is a good self-manager, then he or she is more likely to be able to manage other people.

Managing yourself is very much about the skills of managing:

- your self-confidence
- conflict which arises at work, both between yourself and other people (inevitable) and between the members of your team (also, sadly, inevitable)
- stress – which is also inevitable and arises out of the process of just getting on with your job and living your life
- time – which is a finite resource and which can be used effectively, but which can't be stretched (there are only 24 hours in a day and 7 days in each week, no matter how powerful or important you are)

In this Workbook we are going to focus, in detail, on these important self-management skills which will enable you to work more confidently, more efficiently and more effectively.

Objectives

By the end of this Workbook you should be able to:

- Apply techniques to ensure a positive, assertive approach
- Use a range of skills to deal with difficult people and manage different types of conflict situations
- Understand the nature of stress and apply techniques for stress management
- Effectively manage your time

Section 1 The assertive manager

Introduction

Assertive communication is a key management skill. Many people are unclear about assertiveness and often confuse being 'assertive' with being 'aggressive'.

Assertiveness is about stating your opinions honestly and directly. It's also about being able to ask for what you want, saying what you don't want and having the courage to say 'No' when 'No' feels right and appropriate.

In this section of the Workbook we shall be looking at ways in which you can develop assertive communication skills, regardless of the situation in which you find yourself, or the people with whom you have to deal.

The power of self-confidence

Self-confidence is that almost indefinable quality which makes such a significant difference to the way we run our lives. Like some curious 'factor X', you will certainly know those times when you have it, and those times when you don't have it. You will immediately recognize it in others, and from time to time, if you are like most people, you will find yourself wishing you had more of it. But what, exactly, is self-confidence?

When you are self-confident you will feel and behave in certain ways that signal, both to you and to the rest of the world, that you feel good about yourself. When asked to describe that self-confident feeling, a number of senior managers made the following comments:

1 'When I'm feeling confident I'm prepared to tackle more or less anything that comes up. I know that no matter what happens I'll be able to cope – one way or another.'

2 'When my confidence is high I look forward to new and challenging situations. It's as though I know that even if something doesn't work out, I won't fall apart. It might be a setback, but it won't be the end of the world.'

3   'I feel able to start new projects, meet new people, take risks. I don't put things off because I'm worried about failure. I just go for it.'

4   'I feel good about myself – as though I have value. I feel that what I have to say may not always be right, but that it's as valid and important as anything other people might have to say.'

When those same managers were asked to describe their view of themselves when they were lacking in confidence, their answers were very different:

1   'When I'm not confident I feel very unsure about my ability to do things – especially new things. Even though I know, at an intellectual level, that I've got the necessary skills and experience I just doubt my own ability ... in fact, I feel sure that I'll make a total mess of everything.'

2   'When my confidence is low I sometimes feel paralysed by indecision. I don't want to take the initiative because I feel sure that I'm going to get it wrong, so it's better to do nothing.'

3   'When I'm lacking self-confidence I just want to stay with the familiar ... projects, people, situations, whatever. I try to avoid anything that might be viewed as confrontational ... because at those times I always feel sure that other people will get the better of me.'

4   'When I don't feel confident I'm very unsure of myself. I tend to keep my views to myself, I find it very hard to say no, and if I come up against someone who is in self-confident mode I always give way.'

The activity below will give you an opportunity to think about the events and people which affect your confidence.

ACTIVITY 1

Answer the following questions honestly, as they will help you to understand who and what is most likely to impact on your confidence. To preserve confidentiality, you may prefer to write your answers to the questions on a separate sheet of paper.

1   In what circumstances do you feel most confident?

2a Who are the people who make you feel most confident?

2b What do these people say or do to increase your confidence?

3   When do you feel least confident?

4   What is it that causes you to lose confidence? Which situations or people?
    Which actions or attitudes?

FEEDBACK

For everyone, confidence comes and goes. We all have periods in our lives when we feel highly confident, sometimes even over-confident.

OVER-CONFIDENCE

Periods during which you were over-confident may have been experienced as times when you were adamant that you knew best and were totally unwilling to listen to alternative viewpoints and opinions. By refusing help and disregarding advice you may have found yourself launched on a solitary pathway to disaster. Or maybe you were unrealistic about your capabilities, or you accepted more than your fair share of responsibility and then found yourself drowning in a sea of paperwork.

LOW CONFIDENCE

Many managers have commented that at times of low confidence they find themselves asking the silent question: 'When will they find out that I can't really do this, and I'm not as good as they think I am?' When we are lacking in confidence we doubt our abilities and assume (wrongly) that everyone else doubts our abilities too.

CONFIDENCE

Confidence is usually experienced as a feeling that we can cope, and accept challenges, take risks and deal with life realistically.

THE SELF-CONFIDENCE CYCLE

The usual cycle for most people is to experience a period of over-confidence, followed by a trough of low confidence. Then, after a time, we recover and soldier on, our confidence growing little by little as we prove, to ourselves and others, that we are capable people, after all. See Figure 1 below.

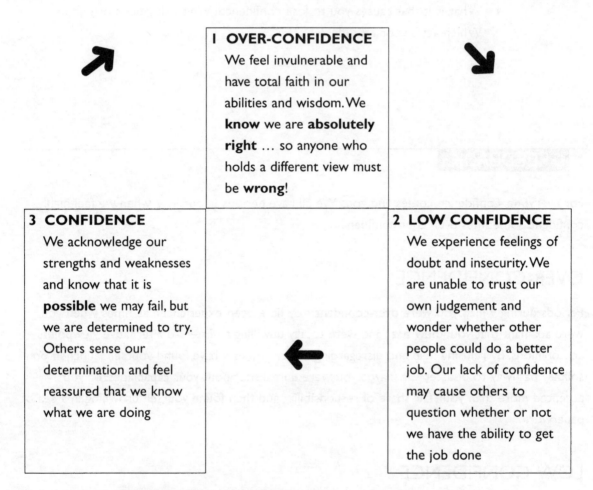

1 OVER-CONFIDENCE
We feel invulnerable and have total faith in our abilities and wisdom. We **know** we are **absolutely right** ... so anyone who holds a different view must be **wrong**!

3 CONFIDENCE
We acknowledge our strengths and weaknesses and know that it is **possible** we may fail, but we are determined to try. Others sense our determination and feel reassured that we know what we are doing

2 LOW CONFIDENCE
We experience feelings of doubt and insecurity. We are unable to trust our own judgement and wonder whether other people could do a better job. Our lack of confidence may cause others to question whether or not we have the ability to get the job done

Figure 1   The self-confidence cycle

Your answers to the previous activity should have highlighted for you those particular people and circumstances which either build or destroy your inner sense of purpose, value and competence.

The keys to building and maintaining a steady and constant level of self-confidence are:

■ Recognize that **no-one** is confident all the time, even though they may **appear to be**

■ Avoid comparing yourself to other people. They have their competences, you have yours

■ Acknowledge your own strengths, skills and abilities

■ Learn and constantly practise assertive behaviour
■ Always remember that if you **look** confident and **sound** confident, that's how people will perceive you (They will have no idea about what's going on inside your head.)

What's your style?

Every moment of every day, at home and at work, you choose the way you respond to people and situations. In most situations, your response will be either:

■ aggressive
■ non-assertive, or
■ assertive

You may find yourself choosing to operate within one of these modes of behaviour most of the time, or you may find yourself responding aggressively sometimes, with some people; non-assertively sometimes, with some people, and assertively at other times, with other people. You may be perfectly happy with this state of affairs, or you may, like most people, wish that you could be more in control of your feelings and your responses. If this is the case, the first step to changing the way you behave is to understand the differences between these three modes of behaviour.

ACTIVITY 2

What do you think are the differences between aggressive, non-assertive and assertive behaviour? For each of the headings below, give three examples of behaviour or communication.

Aggressive behaviour and communication:
1
2
3

Non-assertive behaviour and communication:
1
2
3

Assertive behaviour and communication:
1
2
3

AGGRESSIVE BEHAVIOUR

Examples of *aggressive* behaviour include:

- putting your own needs first, every time
- getting your own way, no matter what you have to do to achieve your objective
- making it very difficult for other people to hold a different opinion
- refusing to listen because you **know** you are **right**
- using verbal or physical intimidation such as shouting, swearing, staring, throwing papers around, slamming doors
- taking advantage of people who are behaving non-assertively
- manipulating people to get your own way

Tony, a senior manager in a teaching hospital, explains his use of aggressive behaviour:

I'm someone who likes to get things done – if there's a decision to be made, let's make it and move on … and I used to get really impatient with people who like to think things through and work more slowly. At meetings I'd push and push and eventually force the team to agree with me. I felt that I was right, and it seemed just a waste of time to spend three hours considering all the possible options and discussing all the 'maybes' and 'what ifs'. I really didn't feel I was being aggressive, I just thought I was being an efficient and effective manager … until it all blew up in my face! I pushed something through and it went very, very wrong. The team took great delight in describing, in excruciating detail, how I had been in the driving seat – refusing to listen, refusing to discuss the options. I had to agree … and then look at how I could change my approach. It isn't easy – because I still want to push on when things slow down, but I have to admit that there's been a significant improvement in the way the team performs.

NON-ASSERTIVE BEHAVIOUR

Examples of *non-assertive* behaviour include:

- deliberately avoiding disagreements
- backing down when faced with aggressive behaviour
- putting up with situations which annoy or frustrate you when you could, in fact, do something about it
- saying 'yes' when you really want to say 'no'
- not being honest about how you feel, and not asking for what you want in case others get angry or upset, or think badly of you
- ignoring your own needs and wishes
- always putting other people first
- putting yourself down, either by making jokes about your ability or by making unnecessary apologies

David, MD of a precision engineering company, explains his use of non-assertive behaviour:
My background is non-technical and non-scientific. I understand trends and marketing and I can spot a good business opportunity; those are my strengths. Because of the nature of the business we have a number of very highly qualified people working here ... I call them The Boffins. They're very bright, very good at what they do ... and I always feel disadvantaged because they know more about the technical side of things than I do. I find myself agreeing with people when I really want to say 'No! That's not what I want.' Instead, I say 'Yes' – because I feel they know more than I do – and then find myself burning with frustration because I've done it again!

ASSERTIVE BEHAVIOUR

Examples of *assertive* behaviour include:

- communicating your needs, wishes, feelings and opinions calmly, clearly, directly, honestly and factually
- recognizing that **everyone** (this means you **and** the rest of the world too) has the right to hold their own views and opinions
- recognizing that other people may operate in a different way to you, and allowing them to work in their own way, at their own pace
- listening carefully to other people, even when you disagree
- saying 'no' when you choose to
- wanting to reach a workable solution and accepting that this may involve a compromise
- choosing to behave non-assertively when this is the most appropriate action to take

Carole, Operations Director in the leisure industry, describes her experience of using assertive behaviour:

I used to see-saw between being non-assertive and aggressive. I had great difficulty expressing my views and feelings because I felt it was important to keep things 'nice' and 'calm' on the team. I didn't want confrontations or disagreements and I suppose I also felt, as a woman manager, that if I opposed the majority view, then I could be perceived as difficult or argumentative. So I would go along with things and inwardly become more and more angry and upset. And then I'd blow! I'd really lose my temper over some minor problem, and all the frustration I'd been holding in would spill out ... it wasn't very pleasant and it certainly wasn't professional. Now that I've learned what being assertive means I feel able to calmly put my point of view and negotiate for a compromise which suits everyone. And, because I know I have those skills, I can afford to be non-assertive when the situation calls for it. For example, I recently went to a meeting with a new and very important client. He behaved abominably to everyone – he was rude and aggressive and totally unreasonable. In the past I would have taken it ... and then felt really bad about the situation afterwards. On this occasion I weighed up the situation, decided that walking away with a signed contract was my key objective and number one priority ... and I so I kept quiet and smiled a lot. That was OK because I achieved my goal ... and I felt absolutely fine because I had made a conscious choice to behave the way I did. I think, at subsequent meetings, this person was more than a little surprised at the change in my style, to say the least!

Use the next activity as an opportunity to think about your responses to a variety of different work situations.

ACTIVITY 3

Consider the questions below and then tick the box which most clearly describes the frequency with which you display this behaviour.

	Always	Often	Now and Then	Never
1 I have difficulty dealing calmly with angry people	❏	❏	❏	❏
2 I find myself becoming quite angry if I feel that people are trying to take advantage of me – and I let them know	❏	❏	❏	❏
3 When my views or actions are challenged I feel intimidated	❏	❏	❏	❏
4 Because it is important to me that people hold a good opinion of me I tend to go along with the majority view	❏	❏	❏	❏
5 I prefer a peaceful life, and don't like to make waves	❏	❏	❏	❏
6 In difficult situations I am able to control my emotions and hold my ground	❏	❏	❏	❏
7 I like to be in control of what's happening	❏	❏	❏	❏
8 There are some people who have the knack of making me feel inadequate – and I find myself agreeing with them when I would really prefer not to	❏	❏	❏	❏
9 I can be volatile and quick-tempered when things aren't going my way	❏	❏	❏	❏
10 I make a real effort to seek a win/win outcome	❏	❏	❏	❏

		Always	Often	Now and Then	Never
11	I consider that what I have to say is equally as important as anything anyone else might have to say	❏	❏	❏	❏
12	I can say no to colleagues and subordinates, but I find it hard to say no to someone who has power over me	❏	❏	❏	❏
13	I have the confidence to ask for what I want – even if I might risk upsetting someone else	❏	❏	❏	❏
14	In business, the end justifies the means, and I do whatever I think is necessary	❏	❏	❏	❏
15	I think good teamwork depends on a harmonious working atmosphere – so I go out of my way to avoid disagreeing with colleagues	❏	❏	❏	❏
16	I can bite the bullet and say what I think, honestly and directly	❏	❏	❏	❏
17	When problems occur, I automatically assume responsibility for causing the problem	❏	❏	❏	❏

FEEDBACK

- If you responded with **always** or **often** to questions 1, 2, 7, 9, 14, then you are likely to be adopting a fairly aggressive attitude in your working relationships.
- If you responded with **always** or **often** to questions 3, 4, 5, 8, 12, 15, 17, then you are likely to be responding to work situations with a fairly non-assertive attitude.
- If you responded with **always** or **often** to questions 6, 10, 11, 13, 16, then you are likely to be responding to work situations with assertive behaviour and communication.

Whichever type of behaviour you normally adopt, whether aggressive, non-assertive or assertive, your style has consequences for you, your work colleagues and the people with whom you share your life.

ACTIVITY 4

For each mode of behaviour – aggressive, non-assertive and assertive – consider the ways in which this approach might impact on you, your colleagues and work situations.

Aggressive behaviour

(a) List two consequences which your aggressive behaviour might have for you personally:

1

2

(b) List two consequences which your aggressive behaviour might have upon your colleagues:

1

2

(c) List two consequences which your aggressive behaviour might have upon work situations:

1

2

Non-assertive behaviour

(a) List two consequences which your non-assertive behaviour might have for you personally:

1

2

(b List two consequences which your non-assertive behaviour might have upon your colleagues:

1

2

(c) List two consequences which your non-assertive behaviour might have upon work situations:

1

2

Assertive behaviour

(a) List two consequences which your assertive behaviour might have for you personally:

1

2

(b) List two consequences which your assertive behaviour might have upon your colleagues:

1

2

(c) List two consequences which your assertive behaviour might have upon work situations:

1

2

FEEDBACK

THE CONSEQUENCES OF YOUR AGGRESSIVE BEHAVIOUR

These can be long-term and potentially quite serious, both for you and everyone around you. They include:

■ health problems such as ulcers, hypertension, migraine, exhaustion
■ feelings of guilt or regret
■ breakdown of communication
■ loss of trust and respect
■ isolation from colleagues and friends
■ short-term and long-term damage to projects resulting from :
    − shortage of information: people are unwilling to confront you with the truth because they know how you are most likely to react
    − shortage of specialist knowledge: you haven't given people a genuine opportunity to contribute
    − limited access to the grapevine
    − inability to call in 'favours': you don't help anyone, so why should they help you?
■ short-term and long-term damage to career prospects

If you regularly use aggressive behaviour, you may reap short-term rewards, such as getting your own way or achieving power over others. The down side is that people will seek to avoid you and, wherever possible, they will make sure that you are excluded from developmental projects which require a creative and organic approach. Ultimately, people will work against you.

THE CONSEQUENCES OF YOUR NON-ASSERTIVE BEHAVIOUR

These can be equally serious, and include:

■ health problems, such as depression, lower back pain, digestive problems, insomnia
■ feelings of anger, frustration and self-pity
■ a downward spiral of low confidence and low self-esteem
■ loss of respect
■ breakdown of work relationships as people realize that they are able to take advantage of you ... and then they feel guilty
■ short-term and long-term damage to projects resulting from:
  – missed deadlines: your inability to say no means that you, (and your team) take on unrealistic amounts of work and then are unable to complete on time
  – soaring costs: if you aren't able to deal with aggressive colleagues, spending can quickly get out of control, or you can find yourself burdened with many 'nice' but expensive and unnecessary resources
  – poor teamwork: your inability to take a firm line with aggressive colleagues may lead to squabbles, arguments, confrontations and, ultimately, a total breakdown of working relationships on the team
  – ill-conceived ideas: because you find yourself unable to control aggressive colleagues you could find yourself held responsible for an outbreak of expensive mistakes resulting from people realizing they can be as outrageous and experimental as they like
■ short-term and long-term damage to career prospects

If you regularly use non-assertive behaviour you may often reap short-term rewards, such as avoiding unpleasantness or keeping everyone happy. The down side is that you will become increasingly frustrated and anxious as people begin to assume that you will agree to their demands. You will feel that you are losing control and that your preferences, opinions and ideas carry little weight with the team.

THE REWARDS OF ASSERTIVE BEHAVIOUR

The benefits include:

■ fewer stress-related health problems
■ improved self-confidence, self-esteem and self-respect
■ increased respect from others
■ improved work relationships as people begin to:
  – gain confidence in your honesty and openness
  – realize that you say what you mean, and mean what you say
  – recognize that you are a 'safe pair of hands'
  – know where they stand
  – feel free to make suggestions and offer up creative ideas
  – willingly share information

- short-term and long-term benefits for projects include:
  - consistent achievement of objectives: because all your agreements are realistic, deadlines are met and spending remains within budget
  - improved teamwork: the aggressive people realize that they will not be able to intimidate you, the non-assertive people recognize they will be listened to. Everyone begins to understand that you are prepared to discuss, negotiate and – where necessary – compromise
- short-term and long-term career benefits

People begin to realize that you have the confidence to voice your opinions and ideas reasonably and calmly. They come to see you as someone who will not be intimidated or manipulated; who will work at creating harmonious relationships and who operates with a high degree of firmness, integrity and honesty.

Assertive behaviour in action

Being assertive involves operating from a position where you recognize that:

- you have the right to be heard **and so does everyone else**
- you have the right to hold your own views, opinions and beliefs **and so does everyone else**
- you have something to contribute **and so does everyone else**
- you have the right to disagree and to say 'no' **and so does everyone else**

The aggressive position is, generally, '**I alone have these rights**', whilst the non-assertive position is '**Everyone has these rights … except me**'.

ASSERTIVE COMMUNICATION

Assertive communication consists of three simple steps which are shown in Figure 2 below.

Step 1 Listen and acknowledge that you have heard and understood the other person's point of view. Ask open questions if you need more information

Step 2 Express, clearly and calmly, your own position and feelings

Step 3 Make constructive suggestions about what could or should happen next

Figure 2 The three steps involved in assertive communication

Step 1 Demonstrate that you've heard and understood

The first step in the process involves making a clear and simple statement which acknowledges whatever has been said. This is important because, if you are dealing with an aggressive person who feels that what they have said has been ignored or brushed aside, then they will become even more aggressive. Non-assertive people will have great difficulty in repeating their question or request, but will inwardly burn with anger and frustration. This can prove to be an explosive combination which may ignite sometime in the future, when you are least expecting it.

Step 2 Express your own feelings and views. Find out more, if you need to

Be direct and honest, and don't be frightened to use 'I' and 'my' statements like:

- 'I'd like it if ...'
- 'I'd prefer it if ...'
- 'I think that ...'
- 'I feel ...'
- 'In my opinion ...'
- 'My view is that ...'

Don't jump to conclusions, and be prepared to take the time to find out more. Ask open how? why? what? when? and where? questions like:

- How do you think we should deal with this?
- What, in your view, is the main problem?
- What changes would you like to see?
- What would your approach be?

Even if someone's opinions are diametrically opposed to yours, do remember that they have the right to hold their own opinions. But also remember that being assertive is about maintaining your own position, even when someone is being aggressive and pushing you hard.

Step 3 Make constructive suggestions as to what might happen next

Often it's not enough just to say 'No' or 'That's not what I want'. Be prepared to make suggestions or offer alternatives. For example:

- 'My view is that we have to proceed very carefully with this, but we could think about ...'
- 'I feel that right now would be the wrong time to launch a new campaign. Even so, I recognize your concern, and it would be helpful to know if you think there

is another time, later this year, when we could introduce these new ideas.'

- 'I'm very concerned that you haven't been able to meet the deadline we agreed. The key step we need to take now is to create a plan to make sure that the job is finished by the weekend. What do you suggest?'

ACTIVITY 5

For the purpose of this activity, imagine that a colleague has said to you:

'I've been thinking about your proposal for upgrading our customer response times and, to be honest, I just don't think it's going to work. I've come up with a different system and I'm going to put it to the board tomorrow … you don't mind, do you?'

1 How might you respond **aggressively**?

2 How might you respond **non-assertively**?

3 How might you respond **assertively**?

FEEDBACK

'I've been thinking about your proposal for upgrading our customer response times and, to be honest, I just don't think it's going to work. I've come up with a different system and I'm going to put it to the board tomorrow … you don't mind, do you?'

This is a fairly aggressive approach, and an aggressive response might well be something like:

'Oh, so you don't think it's going to work! Well, let me tell you that I've spent a lot of time and effort on these proposals and neither you nor anyone else is going to spoil my presentation tomorrow. So, in a nutshell, yes, I do mind – very much. So don't even think about attempting to hijack my work.'

A person using a non-assertive approach would probably say something like:

■ 'Oh … well, I suppose there'll be enough time …'

or even

■ 'I'm sorry you think my proposals are so dreadful – perhaps you ought to make the presentation instead of me.'

Someone using assertive communication might say:

■ 'The board is expecting me to make my presentation at 3.15 and I expect to talk about my proposals for at least forty-five minutes. As the meeting is due to end at four o'clock there just won't be time for you to make your points. I think it would be better if you could talk to Tom and set up another meeting when you'll have sufficient time to explain your plans in detail.'

Core statements

Working out your core statement can be a very useful exercise when you know, in advance, that you have to:

■ confront someone and explain your dissatisfaction
■ stand firm to your point of view in the face of strong opposition
■ ask for something you want
■ refuse a request

To create a core statement, simply focus on your objective. Think about what you want to achieve as a result of the communication. Here are some examples of core statements which match the list given above.

CONFRONT SOMEONE AND EXPLAIN YOUR DISSATISFACTION

■ 'I'm extremely concerned by your sales figures to date and I need to see an improvement by the end of the month.'
■ 'I feel that the way you answered questions at that meeting was inappropriate and unacceptable because you used out-of-date statistics. I would like you to update your information and then arrange another meeting so we can go through the data again.'
■ 'I've noticed that your team is not producing the results that we agreed would be a minimum acceptable level of performance. I'd like you to prepare a report, by Wednesday, outlining the steps you will take to improve performance.'

STAND FIRM TO YOUR POINT OF VIEW IN THE FACE OF STRONG OPPOSITION

- 'I understand your concerns, but I am convinced, having seen the lab report, that we have no alternative but to abandon the project.'
- 'I can see this is important to you, but, in my opinion, the plan won't work because there isn't enough in the budget to cover all the additional costs.'
- 'I can see why you think we ought to wait, but, in my opinion, if we're going to do this, we need to do it now before we lose our competitive edge.'

ASK FOR SOMETHING YOU WANT

- 'I recognize that money is tight, but I really need another member of staff if we're to reach the targets we've agreed.'
- 'I know there have been difficulties in the past, but I really need to spend some time in the Amsterdam plant, if I'm going to find a solution to the problem.'
- 'I can see why you don't want another delay, but, in my opinion, further tests are absolutely necessary because I need to make sure that the network will support the software.'

Your core statement should be your bottom line, ideal outcome. Of course, as part of the process of searching for a win/win outcome you may have to negotiate and, to some extent, compromise. But, at the very least, if you give your core statement some serious thought **before** the encounter, you will have a clear idea of what you want the outcome to be.

Use the next activity as an opportunity to create a core statement which you can use in a work-related situation.

ACTIVITY 6	C5.3

Think about a current work-related situation in which you need to use an assertive approach. Take the opportunity to tackle the situation assertively and then complete the boxes below.

1   Provide a brief description of the situation.

2   What is your core statement? (This should reflect your ideal outcome.)

3   How many times did you use your core statement?

4   What was the final outcome, and how does this compare to your core statement?

Saying 'no!'

Many people have great difficulty with refusing requests and saying 'No!' An aggressive refusal to a reasonable request can cause terrific resentment: 'I only asked if I could move my office and she went ballistic!' A non-assertive refusal can leave the petitioner wondering whether the answer was yes or no: 'I went in, asked if I could change the schedules, he rambled on for nearly twenty minutes and I've come out of his office and I still don't know. What a waste of time!'

ACTIVITY 7

List four reasons why people might feel reluctant to say 'No!'

1
2
3
4

FEEDBACK

People often mistakenly believe that if they say no, people will:

- get angry and cause a scene
- feel resentful and, at a later date, take some kind of revenge
- spread gossip and rumour about the refusal
- perceive the person saying 'no' in a very negative way

Robin, a Process Engineer, explains:

I just hate having to say No. I always feel guilty, and I always think that people will feel angry or let down if I refuse a request. So I can never really win. If I say No, I feel guilty or anxious … and I always seem to spend ages apologizing. If I say Yes, I often feel irritated or frustrated because, afterwards, I wish I'd had the courage to say No. It's hopeless.'

If you are caught in a similar spiral, the key points to remember are:

- When you say 'No', you are merely refusing the request and not rejecting the person
- Refusals can be simple, open and honest statements

NO, WITH A REASON

If you feel it is appropriate, you can soften your refusal by giving a reason for saying no:

- 'No, I can't approve an increase to your budget *because* I'm waiting for the results of the internal audit'
- 'No, I can't extend the deadline *because* the client has to ship the delivery on Thursday'

NO, WITH AN ALTERNATIVE

Offering an alternative is another technique you can use when you feel that a straightforward no might be inappropriate, for example when dealing with an important client or a very senior colleague.

'No, I can't promise that I'll be able to meet your deadline. I can, however, assure you that I can complete the project by the 22nd'
'No, I don't feel that that approach would get the results we need. What I would like to suggest is that we talk to the legal department before we make a decision'

SIMPLE NO

Sometimes a simple, straightforward no is all that is required. Don't apologize and don't beat around the bush. Just calmly and clearly say 'No'.

- 'No, I'm not prepared to authorize that expenditure'
- 'No, I'm not willing to agree to that'

BROKEN RECORD NO

The broken record is a useful technique when you find yourself dealing with manipulative or aggressive people who will simply not take no for an answer. In some situations you will find it useful to work out what your core statement is before you get involved in the conversation.

You: **No, I can't promise that I'll be able to meet your deadline.** I can, however, assure you that **I can complete the project by the 22nd.**

Client: But you've never let me down before!

You: And I don't intend to let you down this time. **I can't promise that I can meet your deadline** because the specification has been changed and it's now very complex. I can promise that **I can complete the project by the 22nd.**

Client: But surely, if you pull out all the stops, get extra people in …

You: Because the specification has been changed the nature of the project has changed. If we had stayed with the original ideas I could have completed in time to meet your deadline. But now **I can't promise to do that. I can finish and deliver by the 22nd.**

Client: But the contract states that the project will be done by the 9th.

You: Yes, you're right. But the contract describes the original specification. The new specification requires a great deal more work, and **I can't promise to finish by the 9th, which was the original deadline. I can assure you that I can deliver everything, to your new specification, by the 22nd.**

The key points to remember, when using the broken record technique, are to keep your nerve and continue to repeat your core statement.

Your rights

As we have already mentioned, everyone (that means you **and** the rest of the world) has certain rights. These are shown in Figure 3 below, and you may find it helpful, as part of your assertiveness strategy, to photocopy the list and keep it beside your desk as a constant reminder.

You have the right to

- **say No**
- **express your views, opinions and beliefs** (even if they are different from the mainstream)
- **ask for what you want** (while recognizing that you might not always get it)
- **change your mind** (in the light of new information or circumstances)
- **make mistakes** (because everyone does)
- **not know or understand** (because you can't be expected to know and understand everything)
- **make your own choices** (because you know what you need and what suits you best)
- **be yourself**

Figure 3

Assertive body language

When practising assertiveness, you need to make sure that your attitude, words and non-verbal communication all match. Body language is a powerful form of communication. If, for instance, you say something like 'I'm not prepared to support you on this one', while at the same time smiling a sickly smile and wringing your hands, then your listener will know that he has got you in a tight corner.

ACTIVITY 8

List three examples of assertive **non-verbal** communication:

1

2

3

FEEDBACK

There are a number of body language signals you can give to show that you are prepared to listen, but you really do mean what you say. These include:

- standing or sitting upright and straight
- not fidgeting. By keeping your movements to a minimum you will give an impression of calmness and authority
- looking the other person squarely in the eye without staring. Staring is aggressive, and being unable to make eye contact is often perceived as non-assertive, or even shifty
- matching the expression on your face to the words you are using. A stony, impassive face can be aggressive, and a hesitant or fixed smile can be perceived as inappropriate and non-assertive
- maintaining an even, well modulated tone of voice. Shouting, or speaking very softly and very slowly through clenched teeth are aggressive techniques. Non-assertive people often speak hesitantly and allow their words to trail away at the end of sentences

The next activity will give you an opportunity to record your progress as an assertive manager.

ACTIVITY 9   C5.3

This activity is designed to help you to keep a journal of work-related events and situations where you need to use assertiveness skills. You may decide to complete and leave the journal sheet in this Workbook, or you may prefer to photocopy the sheet and, for the sake of confidentiality, keep them in a separate folder.

Situation I Give a brief description of the situation, together with your reasons for choosing to use assertiveness skills. Include a note of your core statement.

Encounters Briefly describe your encounters with other people involved in the situation. Include a note of their approach (aggressive, non-assertive, assertive) and your responses.

Outcome Briefly describe the outcome of the situation and the way in which this compares with your core statement.

Key learning points Note down the key learning points you have gained from this situation. What went well? What was difficult? What will you repeat in the future, and what will you avoid? If you had the opportunity to re-run the same situation all over again, what might you do differently?

Summary

- The keys to building self-confidence are:
  - recognize that no-one is self-confident all of the time (even though they may appear to be)
  - avoid comparing your skills and competences with other people's
  - acknowledge your own skills, strengths and abilities
  - learn and constantly practise assertive behaviour
  - if you look and sound confident, others will believe that you are confident
- Aggressive behaviour is demonstrated by:
  - putting your own needs first and doing whatever it takes to get your own way
  - making it impossible for other people to hold a different opinion

- using verbal or physical intimidation – shouting, swearing and so on
- Non-assertive behaviour is demonstrated by:
  - putting up with annoying and frustrating situations because you don't want to 'make waves'
  - saying yes, when you really want to say no
  - ignoring your own needs and wishes and always putting other people first
  - going out of your way to avoid disagreements
- Assertive behaviour, which stems from self-confidence, is demonstrated by:
  - communicating your wishes, opinions and feelings openly, honestly and directly. Saying what you mean, and meaning what you say
  - recognizing that you have rights, and everyone else has those rights too
  - saying 'No' when you choose to
  - wanting to reach a workable solution and a win/win outcome
- Assertive communication involves:
  - **Step 1**: Listening and discussing. Asking questions to make sure you understand
  - **Step 2**: Expressing, calmly and clearly, your own views and opinions. Using 'I' and 'my' statements
  - **Step 3**: Making constructive suggestions about what could happen next
- A core statement is a brief description of the outcome you hope to achieve when you need to:
  - confront someone
  - maintain your position or point of view
  - ask for something
  - say no
- Techniques for saying 'No':
  - No with a reason
  - No with an alternative
  - Simple No
  - Broken record No
- Assertive body language involves:
  - good posture – standing or sitting upright and straight
  - not fidgeting
  - maintaining steady eye contact
  - matching the expression on your face to the words you are using
  - maintaining an even, well modulated tone of voice

Section 2   The conflict manager

Introduction

It is not unusual to hear managers muttering, in the privacy of their car or office, 'This job would be great if it wasn't for the people!' If you have ever uttered these words in a moment of despair, and subsequently felt guilty, don't worry – you're not alone.

Regardless of the type of organization for which you work, one of your key roles will be managing other people. You will also, probably, belong to one or more teams, as a team member. This means that, on a daily basis, there will be countless opportunities for you to either become embroiled in conflict with other people, or have to deal with the conflict which has occurred between other people. The conflicts may be fairly minor – for instance, someone insists on regularly parking in your allocated space, or someone persists in making sarcastic and unprofessional remarks about your ability to do the job. Or they may be potentially very serious – for example, two of your team members become involved in physical violence in the company car park, or team members complain that a colleague is unable to work safely because of substance abuse.

If you are really lucky you may, on average, find yourself having to sort out some kind of conflict once or twice a week. If you are like most managers, then dealing with conflict is a regular, daily occurrence for you. Whether you are personally involved, or merely sorting things out between other people, conflict management will almost certainly affect you, one way or another. Most managers find that, as conflict at work increases, their own stress levels rise. This is often because dealing with the conflict takes up so much time that they have great difficulty in meeting their own job description and achieving their own objectives.

In this section of the Workbook we shall be looking at the most common causes of conflict and the action you can take to manage those situations effectively.

What causes conflict at work?

The main *root* causes of conflict are:

- success
- objectives and beliefs
- territory
- irrational hostility
- personal style

The next activity will give you an opportunity to think about those occasions when you have been drawn into conflict because of these root causes.

ACTIVITY 10   C5.3

1   Cast your mind back to an occasion in your working life when you were obviously successful and your success was, in some way, recognized and rewarded.

(a)   How did your managers, colleagues and subordinates perceive your success?

(b)   In what way did your success affect your working relationships?

(c)   Were there any negative responses? If so, what were they?

(d)   What was the effect of your success on your subsequent job performance?

(e)   What was the final outcome?

2 Think back to a time in your working life when either your objectives or your beliefs have been in conflict with those of your managers, colleagues or subordinates.

   (a) How did you perceive those people whose objectives or beliefs were in conflict with yours?

   (b) To the best of your knowledge, how did they perceive you?

   (c) How did this conflict affect the job performance of everyone involved?

   (d) What was the final outcome?

3 When was the last time you were involved in conflict over territory – e.g. parking space, office space or furniture, equipment, budget allocation or other resources?

   (a) What was the territory which caused the conflict?

   (b) Did you feel that someone was stepping on your territory? Or did someone else think you were invading theirs?

   (c) What was the outcome?

4 When was the last time you took against someone at work for a trivial reason? (maybe their appearance or mannerisms, or perhaps a casual remark to which you took exception).

   (a) What was the cause of your hostility to this person? Was it something they did? Or said? Or the way they looked? Something else?

(b)   How did your hostility manifest itself? How did you behave? How did you communicate?

(c)   Did you ever get over the hostility and resolve the conflict? What was the final outcome?

5   Review the conflict situations in which you have been involved and think about how differences in personal style may have been a contributing factor.

(a)   What differences of personal style were involved? (e.g. Outgoing and charismatic v Plodding and painstaking)

(b)   Would the conflict have occurred if the differences in personal style had not existed?

(c)   Is there a pattern? For example, are there certain types of people with whom you tend to come into conflict?

FEEDBACK

SUCCESS AS A CAUSE OF CONFLICT

Some UK, and many US, companies encourage an atmosphere of healthy competition where *success* is cheerfully recognized and **genuinely** celebrated. In these organizations people who do well are respected, and their contributions are highly valued. Unfortunately, in many UK companies, success – and the energy, drive, ambition and hard work which are the main contributing factors for success – are often viewed in a rather different light. UK managers sometimes perceive successful colleagues as a threat. Success can lead to jealousy and resentment, and these negative attitudes can lead to considerable discord. Cliques and sub-groups can form, consisting of the 'successful' people, and the people who perceive themselves as 'less successful'. Discord can grow into conflict and even, on occasion, turn into a major war between individuals, teams, departments, functions or units of the same company located in different parts of the country. Diana, a conference manager in the hotel industry, explains how her personal success at work caused conflict:

I work for a multinational organization which has hotel and leisure facilities all over the world. About three years ago the company ran a 'suggestions promotion', and the idea was that the person who came up with the best suggestions for improving customer service would be rewarded with an international tour of our flagship properties. I won the trip and went to Hong Kong, Singapore and the States on a working holiday. It was fabulous, and I learned a lot and, of course, came back full of new ideas. I was shocked and very upset to discover the amount of hostility I had to deal with. People with whom I had worked well with **before** *the trip changed dramatically in their attitudes and levels of co-operation* **after** *the trip. Instead of people being pleased for me, and being open to new possibilities for the business, there was petty jealousy and open hostility. It was a very difficult time for me and, although I did manage to stick it out, there were many times I felt like looking around for another job.'*

OBJECTIVES AND BELIEFS AS A SOURCE OF CONFLICT

Within every organization you can expect to find a group of people with different *views, opinions, beliefs* and different personal and work-related *objectives.* This is both healthy and desirable because it leads to a continuous exchange of ideas, an atmosphere of creative competition and an often unspoken 'agreement to disagree'. But different ways of looking at the same task or concept can provide fertile ground for conflict:

- Sylvia's role is to set and control budgets and to make sure that spending stays within the agreed allocations. Mike feels that her approach is too rigid, and her refusal to fund additional resources for his department has, in the long term, cost the company a considerable amount of money. Outcome: **conflict**
- In his spare time Neal is an active member of Greenpeace. He believes passionately in the preservation of the environment and clashes, head-on, with his MD who refuses to sanction more expensive but more environmentally aware working practices. Outcome: **conflict**
- Tim likes to think of himself as a 'New Man' who treats everyone equally and who is perfectly happy to make his secretary a cup of tea. Arthur, Tim's colleague, likes to think of himself as 'one of the lads' and can't see the point of 'all this equal opportunities nonsense'. Outcome: **conflict**

TERRITORY AS A SOURCE OF CONFLICT

Perfectly sane, intelligent and responsible people can lose all sense of proportion when they feel that their territory is being invaded. *Territory* can mean personal space – for instance, an office, a chair, a parking space – but can also mean:

- time
- resources (budget allocations, equipment, staffing)
- pay (salary, overtime, bonus, commission)

- job-related 'perks' (expense account (sandwiches or decent lunch in a good restaurant), car (diesel family saloon or top-of-the-range high-performance vehicle), quality of accommodation and travel, (three-star or five-star hotel: Economy or Business Class), staff (part-time agency temp or full-time graduate personal assistant), communications (phone card or digital mobile phone), technology (standard 486 PC or state-of-the-art Pentium multi-media plus laptop computer with built-in fax and modem for easy access to the Internet))
- responsibilities
- preferred status relationships with important clients or senior management within the company

IRRATIONAL HOSTILITY AS A SOURCE OF CONFLICT

If you are like most people, there will have been times in your life when you have taken an instant dislike to someone, or you've had a deep-seated resistance to do something. If closely questioned, you wouldn't have been able to give a logical reason for your response. You might have muttered, 'He looks shifty', or 'I don't think she's got her mind on the job', or 'He reminds me of my old headmaster' or 'I don't like the sound of the project – it just doesn't feel right.'

Any one of these views could reasonably be described as an *irrational hostility*. They arise out of our perceptions of other people (which can often be wrong) and they colour our feelings towards them:

- Jim reminds you of your headmaster. You didn't have a good relationship with your head-master. You didn't like him, and the feeling was mutual. Jim's resemblance triggers off unhappy memories, and you make the connection (probably erroneously) that the headmaster was like this, so Jim will probably be like this, too!

The key point to remember is that, from time to time, you may feel irrationally hostile towards some people; and others may have these feelings too. They may 'take against' you or other colleagues for no real reason. Irrational hostility, which usually has no real logical or sensible foundation, can often be found at the core of conflict.

PERSONAL STYLE AS A SOURCE OF CONFLICT

Personal style is an amalgamation of attitudes, perceptions, style of communication, personality, habits and ways of doing things. Many leading-edge management thinkers have created systems for dividing people into different types, categories, behaviours and operational styles. Examples of these include:

- learning styles
- management styles
- team roles
- personality

You will come across a number of these in some of the other Workbooks.

In the meantime, use Figure 4 as a rough guide to help you to see how conflict can easily arise between people who have different personal styles.

TRADITIONALISTS	ANALYSTS
■ prefer familiar, safe situations ■ creatures of habit ■ like to have routines and established systems and procedures ■ like to form close, often social, relationships with other team members ■ generally predictable, patient and loyal	■ slow at decision making because they need to analyse, think things through and explore all the options ■ high standards, both for themselves and the other team members ■ generally thoughtful, precise, systematic and highly critical
COMPETITORS	PERFORMERS
■ easily bored by routine ■ motivated by the possibility of success ■ because they thrive on change, are keen to experiment and find new ways of doing things ■ make decisions quickly and easily, and enjoy risk-taking and the thrill of the chase ■ generally confident, impatient, ambitious people who like to get the job done and move on to the next challenge	■ extremely sociable and good with people, they love to charm, persuade and convince ■ prefer people to systems or ideas ■ can be impulsive and often take a slapdash, 'it'll be all right on the night' approach ■ generally optimistic, easy-going, enthusiastic and fun

Figure 4

Examine Figure 4 and note down, in the space below, four areas of conflict which could arise between the four different personal styles; Traditionalists, Analysts, Competitors and Performers.

1

2

3

4

FEEDBACK

In any situation which involved a mix of these four personal styles, there would be numerous opportunities for conflict, such as:

■ Competitors would be keen to get on with making the decision (possibly any decision, just as long as **something** was decided), while the Analysts would want to look at the problem from all angles. Performers wouldn't really care too much about the decision-making process because they really want to get out and about, where the action is. The Traditionalists would be worried that the decision might mean change, and change is difficult for them to deal with

■ Performers are generally optimistic and easy-going and not overly concerned with detail, while Analysts want things to be **right** – and to get things right, you have to do things properly. Competitors are good at initiating but not necessarily good at completing, so any hold-ups (to get things right) would be a source of frustration and irritation

■ Traditionalists like to get on well with people, and so do Performers. But Competitors are more interested in forging ahead with new ideas, and don't really have time for unnecessary socializing

■ Traditionalists are steady and hard-working; Competitors are dynamic and hard-working

■ Performers are people-orientated and they shine in a social setting, whereas Analysts are systems-orientated people who prefer ideas to people

■ Competitors are often addicted to adrenalin and, when things are too quiet, they will proactively look for challenging new horizons. Traditionalists prefer to stick with what they know, and feel uncomfortable with changing goalposts

As someone who will be called upon, from time to time, to manage conflict it is important that you understand how differences in personal style can be the main trigger for interpersonal difficulties. Conflict may arise not because people are being intentionally difficult (although this sometimes can be the case), but just because they are looking at the same picture down different ends of the telescope, seeing the same thing from widely differing points of view.

Symptoms and tactics

Clearly, before you can attempt to resolve conflict you need to be aware that the conflict exists. Sometimes there are overt symptoms and tactics such as:

■ **symptom**: breakdown in communication
■ **tactic**: written complaint about the 'other party' to union or health and safety representative or senior management

Sometimes the symptoms and tactics are much more subtle. Figure 5 identifies the main symptoms of conflict and the tactics which people tend to use in an attempt to 'win'.

Symptoms	Tactics

■ **Communication**
  – arguments, fights and tears
  – excessive politeness and formality
  – cessation of communication
  – proliferation of memos and other paperwork
  – frosty, tense atmosphere
  – request for intervention by senior management
■ **Deterioration in work standards**
  – missed targets
  – non-attendance at meetings
  – clock-watching
  – low morale
  – lack of co-operation without sound reason
	■ **Communication**
	  – distorting the facts by giving one person, team or department one story, and other people an entirely different version
	■ **Red tape**
	  – tying people in knots with red tape so that it becomes extremely difficult for them to do their job ('I want a detailed activity report on my desk every morning')
	■ **Bypassing official channels**
	  – manipulating people in key positions to provide information or authorization ('Ted's already authorized it, so there's nothing for you to do')
	■ **Subtle sabotage**
	  – making sure that errors and indiscretions (or even untruths) are passed on to the right people ('Tania works too hard … and of course since she's had the baby she's just so tired all the time …')

Figure 5   Symptoms of conflict, and the tactics adversaries use in order to 'win'

Trouble-shooting

The bad news is that, as a manager, as soon as you become aware of hostilities – whether directed towards you or another member of your team – it is your responsibility to do something about it. The good news is that if you take the initiative and act promptly and assertively, you can nip it in the bud and prevent a minor conflict from developing into a major crisis.

ACTIVITY 12

Read through the following case studies and note down, for each:
(a) two strategies you should avoid when dealing with these situations and (b)
two strategies you could use to resolve the situations

CASE STUDY 1

You feel that a colleague (a manager from another function who is on the
same grade as yourself) is undermining your position at work. Although there
isn't much that you can specifically put your finger on, comments have been
made by two members of your team to the effect that this colleague has
criticized your ideas and the way in which you are managing an important
project. Your MD has also made a couple of remarks, which suggest to you
that your colleague has been using *subtle sabotage* to raise doubts about your
competence. What are you going to do about it?

(a) Strategies I should avoid when dealing with this situation:

(b) Strategies I could use to resolve this situation:

CASE STUDY 2

Josie, a member of your team, complains to you that Nicholas, another member of the team, is consistently providing incorrect data in the reports he submits to her on a monthly basis. She suggests to you that the inaccuracies are deliberately designed to cause problems for her and increase her workload. You are aware that there has previously been some subtle tension between these two team members. What are you going to do about it?

(a) Strategies I should avoid when dealing with this situation:

(b) Strategies I could use to resolve this situation:

CASE STUDY 3

Your CEO is planning to move the factory to an out-of-town greenfield site. She invites you to a one-to-one meeting and explains that just about everyone in the organization is vigorously resisting the move. She asks you to talk to the staff and the union representatives in order to 'get them to see sense.'

(a) Strategies I should avoid when dealing with this situation:

(b) Strategies I could use to resolve this situation:

FEEDBACK

CASE STUDY I

This is quite a delicate situation because, at this stage, you don't have any real evidence. You have second-hand information provided by your team members (which may or may not be a distortion of the truth), and a couple of chance remarks made by the MD (to which you may well be over-reacting). In these circumstances, strategies to **avoid** include the following:

Confrontation

If, as is often the case, this scenario has been blown up out of all proportion by **other people**, by confronting your colleague you could appear to be insecure (at best) and totally paranoid (at worst).

Collusion or collaboration

Never be tempted to ask other people to gossip or gather evidence on your behalf. Comments like 'Keep your ear to the ground and let me know if he says anything else' are extremely unprofessional. They also have a nasty habit of backfiring.

Retaliation

Just because **you have been told** or **you think** that someone is using subtle sabotage against you is no excuse for responding in similar fashion.

Strategies to **use** include the following:

Watchfulness

Be careful and cautious around this person, and behave, at all times, with the utmost professionalism. Give this person no cause whatsoever to criticize you or your actions. Say nothing, even as a joke, which you would not be happy to have repeated to your MD (or anyone else).

Assertiveness

Behave assertively at all times with this person. Let them see that you are not a soft touch, and that you are comfortable voicing your views and opinions clearly, and with confidence. Let them know, through words and actions, that, in your view, back-biting, rumour-mongering, gossip and good, old-fashioned lies are unethical and unprofessional.

If you do manage to get some concrete evidence – a memo, letter, e-mail, specific comments made in your presence – then act immediately. Keep your temper and ask coolly and calmly for an explanation: 'I notice that you seem to think that I've been mismanaging the Morgan project. I find that very interesting, and I'd like to know more.' If the person involved tries to bluster or bluff, then you can pin them down and assertively ask for details: 'I'd really like to know, specifically, in what way you think I'm mismanaging the project.'

The key point here is that it is often much easier to resolve conflict **between other people** than it is to deal with conflict **between yourself and someone else**. This is because, where others are involved, as a manager you will have very little emotional involvement in the situation. Of course, you will want a speedy resolution so that you can restore harmony and normal working practices, and get the people involved off your back. When you are personally involved, however, things can be very different. Your emotions are likely to be stirred up, and you may feel:

- angry
- humiliated
- highly competitive and determined to win, or even spiteful and malicious towards the other person, ('You're trying to hurt me, so here's a taste of your own medicine')

Retaliation will not help, as it will only serve to escalate the conflict and, in the long run, make matters worse. So what can you do if you find yourself in direct conflict with someone else?

1 **Look for the root cause of the conflict.** The real, underlying reason for the conflict between you and someone else will probably be either success, objectives and beliefs, territory, irrational hostility or personal style.
2 **Deal with the root cause.** Some suggestions as to how you might do this are outlined in Figure 6 below.

Root Cause	Action you can take to resolve the conflict
Your hostility towards another person due to their success	You may feel angry towards someone because they have achieved success and you have not. Bear in mind that you can't turn the clock back and change things. You can't take their success away, and even if you try, you probably won't spoil it for them. Look for ways in which you can benefit from their success and, instead of wasting time and energy getting mad, direct that same time and energy towards getting better. Even if, in your opinion, they don't deserve their success, they did not succeed just to make you feel bad. They did it for themselves. Now you must do it for yourself.
Someone else's hostility towards you due to your success	Their hostility and anger will arise out of disappointment, bitterness, jealousy, shattered dreams … whatever. If you respond by being angry, then you will definitely make matters worse. Try to re-establish a sound working relationship by adopting, whenever possible, a win/win approach. Support them in their own efforts to win success, and recognize their achievements. If this is not possible (for whatever reason), distance yourself. Practise your

Root Cause	Action you can take to resolve the conflict
	assertiveness skills and, no matter what happens, remain utterly professional in all your dealings with this person. Do not, under any circumstances, attempt to retaliate or adopt an I win/You lose approach.
Your hostility towards another person due to their objectives and beliefs	Your hostility will not change what they believe, but it will cause conflict and bad feeling. Agree to disagree, and respect their right to think and feel in whatever way they choose. Remember that if you disagree with someone's objectives or beliefs, you have the **right** to do that. Equally, they have the **right** to hold those objectives and beliefs.
Someone else's hostility towards you due to your objectives and beliefs	Even if someone is angry towards you, or behaving badly because your objectives and beliefs are different to theirs, do remember that you have the **right** to think and feel however you choose. They also have the **right** to disagree with you, and think and feel in different ways. Look for the areas of common agreement and build on those.
Your hostility towards another person due to their invasion of your territory	The key point is that the other person may have no idea that you are so upset because they have used your office, taken your secretary's time, been given a better computer than you … or whatever. These things may be totally unimportant and irrelevant to them, and they will not have any idea of the depth of your irritation or anger. You may want to explain, assertively, that you don't want this to happen again, e.g.: 'By the way, Mike, I'd prefer it if you didn't use my computer when I'm not in the office because I have it configured in a certain way, and I like it to be left like that.'
Someone else's hostility towards you due to your invasion of their territory	Some people are very territorial about certain, specific things which may not be important to you. If the core of the conflict is about territory, recognize that the chair, the job title, the 'special working relationship' or whatever may be terribly, terribly important to the other person. Don't get angry — just recognize the importance to the other person of the territory which is involved.
Your hostility towards another person due to irrational hostility	If you find yourself feeling hostile to someone without a **logical** reason or cause, then the root of the hostility is likely to be **irrational hostility**. Maybe you've taken against them because they talk loudly, or because they wear 'bad taste' clothes, or because they have an irritating laugh, or remind you of someone you once disliked in the past. When **irrational hostility** strikes, take some time to reflect on why this has occurred. Look beyond the immediate surface cause (the voice, laugh, clothes or whatever), and look for the real person. The factor which irritates you may well be a smokescreen the person is using to hide a lack of confidence, or even a desire to impress you.
Someone else's hostility towards you because of irrational hostility	If someone is behaving in a hostile way towards you and you recognize that this is due to an **irrational hostility**, then there is not too much you can do. You have the right to be yourself, and if this person doesn't approve of some

- ■ **Step 1 – Intervene**
  Where conflict exists, it is important to let the people involved know that you know what is going on, and that you intend to take positive action to deal with the problem.
- ■ **Step 2 – Listen and discuss**
  Get everyone involved together, sit them down and listen to **all** sides of the story. Give equal time and attention to everyone and ask questions. Make sure you understand (a) the facts and (b) the perceptions. You can guarantee that, where conflict exists, each person involved will perceive the situation in a different way:

  'It's his fault because …'
  'That's absolute nonsense! It's her fault because …'

  By allowing each person to give his or her views and opinions you will have the chance to hear what each person thinks, and he or she will have the chance to hear what the others involved think, too. This can often be very enlightening for people involved in a conflict situation. No matter what happens, keep calm and remain assertive. Your role is to remain impartial throughout, so don't take sides, give an opinion or allow yourself to become involved in the situation.
- ■ **Step 3 – Make your position clear**
  Be uncompromising about the fact that you want the situation resolved. By all means show that you want a win/win outcome, but take a tough stand and let everyone know that you will not tolerate behaviour or attitudes which are detrimental to the organization, the department or the team.
- ■ **Step 4 – Negotiate a win/win outcome**
  At this stage you are looking for a resolution which is acceptable to everyone. Ask the people involved to say what they would like to see happen. Returning to the situation in Case Study 2, an example of how this might work would be:

Manager:	'So, it seems to me that what Nicholas is saying is that the data is inaccurate because you're asking for the figures before he has time to correlate all the statistics. Is that right, Nicholas?'
Nicholas:	'That's exactly right!'
Manager:	'So, Josie, is there a way around this?'
Josie:	'Well no, not really … I have to get the figures from Nicholas on the 25th because Tom wants them on the 26th, and that's all there is to it!'
Manager:	'Nicholas, what's the latest date for you to gather all the information?'
Nicholas:	'I can't do it before the 26th because I don't get the figures from Barnsley until then.'
Manager:	'So what would be a solution from your point of view?'
Nicholas:	'More time!'
Manager:	'So it seems to me that if you, Nicholas, can get the figures from Barnsley earlier, or you, Josie, can give the figures to Tom later, then we could resolve the problem. Does that make sense?'
Nicholas:	'Well yes …'

Josie:	'Yes – but Tom won't be happy about that!'
Manager:	'Have you asked him?'
Josie:	'Well, no … not exactly …'

Move slowly towards a solution which the conflicting parties will find acceptable. This may involve a measure of compromise, but look for the win/win. Do not attempt to impose a solution – it won't work because the people in conflict won't want it to work. It may be frustrating, and it will almost certainly be time-consuming, but, if you invest time at the start, you will save time later on. Remember, little upsets can grow into major battles if left unattended. Before the meeting ends, make sure that everyone concerned is crystal clear about the agreements which have been made. Leave no room for 'Oh, I didn't understand' or 'I didn't think I was supposed to be doing that'. For example

'OK, so what we've agreed is that Nicholas will ask Barnsley to send the figures on the Internet on the 24th. Josie will explain the situation to Tom and ask if she can submit the figures on the 26th, in the afternoon. Nicholas, you'll work on the data on the 24th and 25th, and Josie, you will prepare the report on the 25th and 26th and submit the final document on the 26th. Are we agreed?'

Do bear in mind that even the most highly intelligent, qualified and experienced people can lose all sense of reason because of:

- success as a source of conflict
- objectives and beliefs as a source of conflict
- territory as a source of conflict
- irrational hostility as a source of conflict
- personal style as a source of conflict

Your role is to provide a *voice of reason*, help people to reach working agreements and then make sure those agreements stick.

- **Step 5 – Monitor the situation**

Unfortunately, you can't just walk away and wash your hands of the whole affair, however much you might like to. Following on from your intervention, you should monitor the situation carefully. You can do this, both formally and informally, through:

   – a formal follow-up meeting (or even a series of meetings), attended by all interested parties
   – informal meetings (management by walking about) just to check how things are going
  If things are working out, you can breathe a sigh of relief and move on. If the conflict has not been totally resolved, then you will need to go back to step 1, intervention, and start the process all over again.

Case Study 3

In Case Study 3 your CEO has asked you to talk to people and 'get them to see sense' or, put another way, 'Get them to agree to do something they don't seem to want to do'. In this situation, strategies to **avoid** include the following:

Appeasing

Don't, **ever**, be tempted to make promises you can't keep, or embellish the truth to turn a situation around. This, when your strategy comes to light, will just make matters worse. You will lose trust and credibility because of your unethical and unprofessional behaviour.

Divide and rule

This is a slightly different version of appeasement, and involves giving different stories to different people, or maybe offering different inducements to get the desired end result.

Serial killer

This strategy involves going in to the situation with 'all guns blazing' and laying down the law: 'This is how it is, and this is how it's going to be. Anyone who doesn't like it can leave now.' People may be stunned into silence by this approach, but you will simply drive the conflict underground and encourage further, and possibly more destructive, conflict.

Strategies to **use** include:

- Listening and discussing
- Giving due consideration to people's concerns
- Negotiating and compromising
- Working towards a win/win outcome
- Allowing people to take ownership of the solution

Knocking heads together, giving in or imposing the law do nothing to solve conflict. But if you help people to reach a solution they feel comfortable with, they will take ownership of the solution and want to make it work. There is no specific formula for this, because every situation is different. The keys to success are communication, assertiveness and patience. Don't lose your temper and click into aggressive mode. Don't allow aggressive behaviour to push you into being non-assertive. Use the list shown in Figure 8 as a checklist to remind you of the key actions to take.

- Listen carefully
- Ask questions and keep on asking until you are sure you understand
- Use open body language
- Use 'I' and 'My' statements
- State your opinions, say what you would like to see happening
- Give everyone else the chance to have their say
- Move, one step at a time, towards agreement
- Search for a win/win outcome where everyone feels they have achieved something which is of benefit to them
- Keep calm and don't lose your temper
- Think before you speak
- Be consistent, fair and even-handed towards everyone
- Don't give in to bullying tactics
- Remember your rights
- Remember everyone else's rights

Figure 8   Assertiveness checklist for conflict resolution

The next activity gives you an opportunity to record your progress in resolving a conflict situation at work.

ACTIVITY 13   C5.1, C5.2, C6.1, C6.2

1 Briefly describe the cause of the conflict.

2 Who is involved in the conflict?

3 What were their positions at the start of the conflict?

4 What steps did you take to check the facts?

5 When and how did you first intervene?

6 What strategy did you use to resolve the conflict?

7 What agreements were reached between the parties at the end of the first meeting?

8 How did you monitor the situation?

9 Did the agreements hold, or was it necessary for you to intervene again? If so, what happened?

10 What was the final outcome?

11 What did you learn from this?

12 What actions would you repeat in the future in a similar situation?

13 What actions would you avoid in the future in a similar situation?

Summary

- The main root causes of conflict are:
    - success
    - objectives and beliefs
    - territory
    - irrational hostility
    - personal style
- The main symptoms of conflict are difficulties with communication and deteriorating work standards. The tactics which are most frequently used in a conflict situation are:
    - distorting the facts
    - using metres of 'red tape'
    - bypassing official channels
    - using subtle sabotage

- Strategies to avoid when seeking to resolve conflict between other people include:
  - blaming
  - ignoring
  - bullying
  - appeasement
  - divide and rule
  - serial killer
- Strategies to use when seeking to resolve conflict between other people include:
  - checking the facts
  - giving due consideration to people's concerns
  - allowing people to take ownership of the solution
- The five-step intervention process consists of:
  1 Intervening
  2 Listening and discussing
  3 Making your position clear
  4 Negotiating a win/win outcome
  5 Monitoring the situation and intervening again, if necessary
- Strategies to avoid when seeking to resolve conflict between yourself and someone else include:
  - confrontation
  - collusion or collaboration
  - retaliation
- When you want to resolve conflict between yourself and someone else, you need to determine and deal with the root cause by keeping an open mind and using assertive communication and behaviour

Section 3 The stress manager

Introduction

Everyone (including and especially managers) gets stressed from time to time. You won't ever totally eradicate stress from your life because stress is usually caused by external situations. So, unless you choose to live alone, on a desert island, with all your needs continuously provided for, there will always be stressful people and situations in your life.

The key to success is learning how to cope with stress. In this section we will be focusing on the factors which create stress, and the tools and techniques you can use to better manage your response to those factors.

Pressure or stress?

Some people thrive on pressure. They actually **need** pressure to help them to make that extra effort to achieve their objectives and to help them feel they are living, rather than just existing. Keith, a partner in a management consultancy, explains:

I enjoy feeling that time is rushing past and I'm chasing after it. I need to be under pressure. When things slow down and get easy, I have to create new situations – challenges, hurdles, whatever you want to call them – otherwise I feel that life is just passing me by. I'm not a laid-back person … I get bored easily and I need constant mental stimulation. I do my best work under pressure … show me an impossible deadline, and I'll show you a happy man.

Some element of pressure is necessary for everyone. People who have little or no pressure in their lives – those with few interests and who are unable to take part in an active social life – are prone to many of the illnesses which affect people with too much pressure. Although the medical profession and stress management experts agree that some pressure is desirable, the problems arise when the pressure develops into stress.

ACTIVITY 14

1   How do you feel when you are working under pressure? List four symptoms
    (mental, emotional or physical) which indicate to you that you are under
    pressure.

    1

    2

    3

    4

2   How do you feel when you are stressed? List four symptoms (mental,
    emotional or physical) which indicate to you that you are stressed-out.

    1

    2

    3

    4

FEEDBACK

THE SYMPTOMS OF PRESSURE AND THE SYMPTOMS OF STRESS

You may have identified some of the following as the symptoms of pressure and stress:

Symptoms of pressure	Symptoms of stress
Feeling:	Feeling:
■ challenged	■ drained
■ excited	■ bored
■ energized	■ exhausted
■ stretched	■ indecisive
■ confident	■ uncertain
■ creative	■ anxious or depressed
■ competent	■ incompetent
■ valued	■ undervalued or neglected
■ powerful	■ powerless
■ moving forward	■ stuck

The excitement of pressure can easily turn into the nightmare of stress, as Anna, a Sales Director, explains.

We were opening up retail outlets all over Europe and I was enjoying every minute of my job – the deadlines, the high-level meetings, the targets – it was great. Then we got some bad press about an environmental issue, and sales started to fall. At that point one of our major suppliers pulled out, and then, on top of everything else my immediate boss, the Sales Director, resigned and I took on his job, together with all his additional responsibilities. The pressure was mounting, and I stopped feeling excited and motivated and started feeling worn-out and quite ill. Then, as if I didn't have enough to cope with, my partner was badly injured in a car accident. Because he works from home as a self-employed consultant I was having to deal with a lot of his work-related issues as well as my own. I was dashing to the hospital, trying to prove myself in a new and even more demanding job, trying to keep his business afloat and trying to do normal, personal things like shopping and paying the household bills. I struggled on for months, not eating, hardly sleeping, getting more and more uptight and irritable and, in the end, I just snapped. I felt totally overwhelmed by it all ... instead of the outgoing, decisive, high-profile person my company needed, I became someone who couldn't make a decision and who, to put it bluntly, couldn't lead a team out of a paper bag.

As well as mental and emotional symptoms, there are a number of stress-related physical symptoms which can sometimes (but not always) signal that pressure has turned to stress. These include:

- eating problems (overeating or loss of appetite)
- sleep disorders (insomnia, wanting to sleep much more than usual or waking up much earlier than usual and not being able to get back to sleep)
- raised blood pressure or palpitations
- nausea and/or vomiting or other digestive problems
- back, shoulder or neck pain which has not been caused by an injury or a pre-existing condition like arthritis
- icy cold hands or profuse perspiration
- frequent and severe headaches

What causes stress?

The most common causes of stress are:
- loss of a partner, child or close family member
- getting married or committing to a long-term personal partnership
- loss of a long-term personal partnership through separation or divorce
- retirement
- difficulties with family, friends or neighbours
- relocation or even moving house in the same area
- taking on large new financial commitments (mortgages, major loans, etc.)

- not being able to meet existing financial commitments
- job loss (redundancy or any other reason)
- job promotion or new/additional work responsibilities
- outstanding personal achievement
- accident, surgery, major illness in the family
- going on holiday
- Christmas

In addition, there are quite specific job-related factors which cause high levels of stress.

ACTIVITY 15

List five factors which cause stress for you at work:

1
2
3
4
5

FEEDBACK

The most common causes of stress at work, for most people, are:

- working environment
- technology
- job role
- relationships
- career development
- change

WORKING ENVIRONMENT

A major stressor can be working in an environment which does not suit your personality or temperament. Some people need to work in a tidy, uncluttered and fairly peaceful environment; some people need a constant change of scenery and a steady stream of new faces and new people with whom to engage; some people need light and fresh air, and so on. A senior manager explains how his working environment played a major role in contributing to his stress at work:

Geoff, Senior Accounts Manager with a precision engineering company:

I need peace and quiet so that I can think clearly. I used to have my own office, and that was fine. Then the company decided to go open-plan, top down ... which meant everyone. I found myself working in a space surrounded by people, ringing telephones, comings and goings and conversations. Even when people whispered it drove me crazy! I ended up taking work home and doing at home – at night and at the weekends – what I was paid to do during office hours. It was a nightmare. I was going to resign – it was that bad. Then I talked to some colleagues and found out that it was having an effect on them too. We had a meeting with the MD and hammered out a compromise which involved setting up some sound-proof screens and re-organizing the desks so that the 'quiet' people all work together. It's fine now.

What can you do to make your work environment less stressful?

First of all, you need to give some careful thought to the kind of environment which suits you best. Do you prefer the mutual support and 'busyness' of an open-plan office? Do you dislike the isolated splendour of a room to yourself? Do you need absolute peace and quiet? Does clutter upset you? Once you have identified whether or not your working environment is causing you stress, then you can start to do something about it. Positive action you could take might include:

- organising additional screening to isolate your desk from the rest of the room
- personally investing in a really comfortable chair which suits you, if you are not able to requisition one from the company
- asking for a telephone which has a flashlight facility, so that you can turn off the ringer bell if the noise is driving you to distraction
- redecorating your office if you are working in dismal or dingy surroundings
- investing one weekend of your time in clearing out the clutter and creating a tidy and streamlined work space

All of these solutions may take some of your personal time or money (if the company is unwilling to meet your requirements). On one level you may feel that this is unacceptable, but if the required changes mean that you will be less stressed, more comfortable and more content at work, then it will be worthwhile.

TECHNOLOGY

Coping with new technology (this might be new plant and machinery or even a fax or laptop computer) with which you feel less than comfortable can be a major source of stress. Neville, a senior partner in a general practice, explains:

We decided, as a Group Practice, to introduce a computer network. This means that all our files are held on computer, and – so the Practice Manager told me – 'we just had to key-in the prescription and hey presto!' Within days I was changed from a highly effective professional into a shambling wreck … I couldn't type, and I just couldn't get to grips with the computer at all. Even worse, all of my disasters were witnessed by my patients, who were sitting in my surgery while I fumbled around. In the end I booked myself onto an evening course and got some serious help. Now, I would hate to be without it – but at the start it was a very different story.

What can you do to make technology less stressful?

Accept that we live in a technological age and it just won't go away. The key to success is learning as much as you possibly can. Take advantage of every possible training opportunity, network with friends and colleagues, or even book yourself onto a part-time evening course at your local college.

JOB ROLE

'Job role' covers everything from the amount of responsibility your job entails and the level of decision making you are empowered to undertake, through to the quantity and quality of resources at your command and the skills-mix of the people on your team. Problems in any of these or similar areas can cause major stress. How one problem leads on to another, in a downward spiral of stress, is illustrated in Figure 9 below.

Lack of skills on the team →	Unable to delegate →	STRESS → ↓	Increase in personal workload →	STRESS ↓
↘ Targets and deadlines not achieved ↓	Insufficient resources →	Targets and deadlines not achieved →	STRESS →	Targets and deadlines not achieved ↓
STRESS ↓	Too much responsibility ↓	Insufficient authority → ↓	STRESS ↓	Lack of support ↓
Loss of credibility →	STRESS →	Loss of confidence →	STRESS →	Targets and deadlines not achieved ↖

Figure 9   How job role factors can cause stress

What can you do to make your job role less stressful?

The first thing to do is to be clear about the boundaries:

- your organization's objectives and priorities
- lines of authority and communication, both above you and below you
- your responsibilities
- the budget and other resources at your command
- your objectives
- your priorities

Then, be prepared to:

- delegate (you don't have to do **everything**)
- where necessary, develop the team (this will leave you free to attend to **urgent and important** tasks)

RELATIONSHIPS

As you have already seen from Sections 1 and 2 of this Workbook, relationships at work have the potential to cause significant stress.

What can you do to make relationships at work less stressful?

The key ways to improve relationships at work are to:

- remember your rights
- respect everyone else's rights
- recognize that you have your own way of working
- respect other people's ways of working
- use assertiveness skills (**say what you mean and mean what you say**)
- negotiate and compromise (look for the **win/win**)

CAREER DEVELOPMENT

Feeling stuck in an undemanding job can be just as stressful as feeling overwhelmed by too much work, too many responsibilities and a wallchart packed with impossible deadlines.

What can you do to make your career development less stressful?

Network, both within your organization and beyond. Let people know that you are prepared to face new challenges. Look for new opportunities and additional responsibilities within your existing company and, if there are none, start looking around for something else.

CHANGE

Just about everyone has some resistance to change. This is because we know we can deal with the familiar – even if it's boring or otherwise unsatisfactory. Change means something new and unfamiliar. 'Will I be able to cope?', 'Will it be worse than it is now?' and 'What'll happen if I don't like it, or I can't do it?' are quite usual responses when change beckons.

What can you do to make change less stressful?

Perhaps the most important and useful thing you can do is to remember that you have already been through many changes in your life, and survived them all. Taking the first step which led you to where you are now probably meant having to deal with some kind of change. You did it then, you can do it again!

The key steps you can take to help you deal with organization change are:

- Get as much information as possible about the proposed changes
- Decide if you need to implement some kind of influencing strategy. If so, plan your campaign and put it into action
- Look for practical ways in which you can overcome any negative aspects you feel you may have identified
- Look for the benefits and see how you can maximize them
- Focus on the positive aspects, rather than the negative

ACTIVITY 16

Complete the chart below by identifying the work-related factors which are stressful for you and the strategies you can implement to either reduce or eliminate the stress:

Cause of stress	Specific stress factors	Action I can take to reduce or eliminate this stress factor
Environment		
Technology		
Job role		
Relationships		
Career development		
Change		

How do you manage your stress?

There's no doubt that, from time to time, everyone gets stressed. And it is also true that everyone, regardless of their circumstances, can take some simple steps to manage that stress. Use the next activity as an opportunity to check whether or not you are already taking the necessary key steps which will help to keep stress to acceptable levels.

ACTIVITY 17

Consider the following questions and complete the chart by ticking the appropriate box.

	Most of the time	Some of the time	Never
I share my worries and concerns with someone I trust			
I have friends with whom I can relax and really be myself			
I take time to be by myself every day, just relaxing and winding down			
I express my feelings and don't just bottle them up			
I have at least one interest or hobby outside of work			
I get involved in activities outside of work which help me to relax			
I can see the funny side of life and enjoy a good laugh			
I take part in some kind of activity which is specifically designed to reduce stress			
I feel reasonably optimistic about the future			
I take some exercise at least once each week			
I'm roughly the right weight for my height, age and build			
I relax and switch off from work by choosing TV or radio programmes, books or music which give me pleasure			
I don't exceed the recommended limits for alcohol consumption (21 units each week for men; 14 units each week for women)			

FEEDBACK

In an ideal situation, in a perfect world, you would be able to answer that you do **all** of these things **most of the time**. Realistically, you should be able to say that you do most of these things **most of the time**. If you found yourself saying that you **never** do **most of these things**, then perhaps it's time to start looking at the way in which stress occurs, and some specific stress management techniques.

Fight or flight?

So far in this Workbook we have looked at some of the causes of stress and some of the effects. Now it's time to take a closer look at the *connection* between the causes and the effects.

In the distant past, we lived in caves and hunted for food. Life was simple, basic and very, very dangerous. Over time, human beings evolved a very sophisticated physical response system which allowed them to react appropriately in dangerous situations and take flight and run away very, very quickly from dinosaurs and sabre-tooth tigers; or stand and fight. We humans developed the *Fight or Flight* to help us to respond to dangerous, life-threatening situations.

We no longer live in caves nor do we hunt for food, but, even now, we still have the physical response system which automatically clicks into place whenever we feel threatened. The way this works is shown in Figure 10 below.

1 Danger You perceive a threat to your safety or well-being. This **could** be a wild animal, but is much more likely to be another driver; an irate customer; a hostile colleague; or a meeting with someone who has power over you. ↓				
		2 The automatic physical response kicks in →		
10 Action stations! Adrenalin and a whole host of associated hormones flood the system, and your body is now ready to run very, very fast, or stand and fight			**3 Heart responds** by beating faster to supply blood more quickly →	**4 Blood responds** Blood pressure rises because the heart is beating faster. Blood clotting agents are released into the bloodstream in anticipation of bleeding from wounds ↓
↑				
9 Digestive system responds Bladder and bowels empty to leave the body lighter	**8 Skin responds** Blood drains away from the surface in order to minimize bleeding from wounds. Perspiration increases in order to cool the body while running or fighting ←	**7 Brain responds** Blood flow to the brain increases in anticipation of the need for quick thinking ←	**6 Liver responds** by releasing cholesterol to provide energy ←	**5 Lungs respond** Breathing rate is increased to ensure a good supply of oxygen ←

Figure 10   The automatic fight or flight response

We become aware of our readiness to deal with danger because we experience the following physical symptoms:

- palpitations
- dizziness
- breathlessness
- cold hands and feet
- perspiration
- vomiting and/or diarrhoea

We are physically ready to run or fight, but the problem is that, in most cases, we are not in a position to do either. Although we have perceived that we are in some kind of dangerous or threatening situation (and this is often subconscious), and our bodies have diligently prepared us to deal with the situation, the reality is usually quite different. Instead, we sit in our cars in a two-mile tail-back and quietly fume. Or we smile through gritted teeth and make assurances that yes, we will bring the project in on time. Or we find ourselves attempting to manage a conflict situation between two warring factions, knowing that we hold the responsibility for finding a win/win outcome.

The end result is that, because of the shots of adreno-cortico-tripic hormone, cortisol, adrenalin and noradrenalin which our body has automatically supplied, we are 'on alert' in a big way. Sometimes we snap, lose our temper, shout and throw things around – then we feel better. Sometimes we bottle it up and pretend we're OK. But if we don't have a technique for clearing these hormones out of our system then, after a while, illness sets in. We can suffer from migraines, ulcers and permanently raised blood pressure. If still nothing is done, the body, tired of being in a constant state of preparedness, can really break down, and strokes, heart attacks and burn-out can be the disastrous result. As Sara Paddison says in her book *The Hidden Power of the Heart*.[1]

Research at London University's Institute of Psychiatry, undertaken over a twenty year period, showed that people who bottled up their emotions under stress were likely to be more prone to cancer. Cigarette smoking or eating foods high in cholesterol by themselves had less effect in causing disease than did negative reactions to stress.

Figure 11 shows the four stages of the stress response.

Developing the habit of using stress management techniques

Anything can become a habit. It usually starts as an activity we do once, then repeat, and then incorporate into our daily or weekly routine. Over time the activity becomes a habit, and we do it without question. For example:

- you take the dog for a walk and go through the park
- you do it again
- every time you walk the dog you go through the park
- you don't really know **why**, but you do it. You don't even question the activity because it has become a habit

Stage 1	Stage 2	Stage 3	Stage 4
We feel threatened	Body and brain prepare to deal with the threat	If we 'fight' or 'take flight', the body utilizes the fats, sugars, hormones and adrenalin which have been released	Hormones, etc. are released and body and brain return to normal

THE DANGER ZONE

⇩   ⇩

Stage 3	Stage 4
We do not 'fight' or 'take flight'. We suppress our emotions. The body does not utilize the fats, sugars, hormones and adrenalin which have been released	We are in a constant state of readiness for 'fight' or 'flight'. Body and brain continue to pump fats, sugars, hormones and adrenalin. Eventually body and brain become exhausted. This leads to illness and, in time, death

Figure 11   The four stages of the stress response

ACTIVITY 18

How do you deal with the stress in your life? What techniques do you use?
Have you developed any stress reduction habits?
List three things you regularly do to help you to manage your stress.

1
2
3

FEEDBACK

There are numerous techniques you can use to manage the 'fight or flight' response. Even if you make only one of these techniques a habit, you will be making a positive move towards managing the stress in your life.

THE EXERCISE HABIT

Some people thoroughly enjoy exercise and make it a habit to do something every week which physically helps the body to release the build-up of 'fight or flight' hormones. On the other hand, many people (especially busy managers) resist the idea of exercise. Here are some options to consider:

- *Swimming* – exercises all the muscles and is kind to aching backs
- *Golf* – a good way of networking
- *Joining a gym* – another good way to meet people and improve your social life
- *Cycling* – needn't be too demanding, and is a good way to get out in the fresh air
- *Dancing* – although often considered a social activity, also a good way to exercise
- *Yoga* – gentle exercise for people of all ages

THE INTERESTS HABIT

It is very easy to become so absorbed in a demanding job that you can find yourself **living to work**, rather than **working to live**. To avoid this trap, you need to get involved in at least one absorbing interest that is not, in any way, work-related. Here are some suggestions:

- Join an evening class to learn something new – perhaps another language, or how to cook Asian food or repair watches
- Take up a hobby which really interests you but for which you have never before allowed time

– photography, redesigning the garden, furniture restoration, painting. Or play chess, do crosswords, write a book, learn to play the guitar

■ Join a book club and aim to read at least one book (which is not work-related) each week

■ Get involved in voluntary work as a means of giving something back to the community

■ Form a 'dinner club' or a 'wine club' with friends and check out the best treats on offer in your area

■ Visit the theatre, the opera, the ballet, museums or art galleries

THE COMMUNICATION HABIT

In her book *He Says, She Says*,[2] Dr Lillian Glass makes the key points:

men and women talk about different things. Women tend to talk about self-improvement, clothes, other people and relationships, while men tend to talk about sports, business, mechanical things, cars and music

Talking things through is a good safety valve because it helps you to explore feelings and emotions. So research suggests that if you are a man, it's time to start talking about personal issues and, if you're a woman, keep talking. Sharing information at a personal level, with someone you trust, is an important stress management tool.

THE 'BE GOOD TO YOURSELF' HABIT

Get into the habit of giving yourself a treat at least once a week. Think of it as a reward for work well done. Here are some possibilities:

■ *Aromatherapy* massage involves the use of essential oils taken from fruit, leaves, flowers and other organic material. Depending on the oil (or combination of oils) which the therapist chooses, the massage can be energizing, balancing, soothing or relaxing

■ *Counselling and psychotherapy* give you the opportunity to explore, through talking, deeply personal issues in a safe, one-to-one environment

■ *Homeopathy* is a well respected branch of alternative medicine which seeks to heal the whole person (mind, body and spirit). Homeopathic medicines (most often prescribed in tablet form) are made from minute amounts of natural, organic substances and can be used to treat physical, mental and emotional problems

■ *Reflexology* is a form of foot massage which helps to balance the emotions and encourages the body to begin the process of repairing any physical damage or disturbance

THE MEDITATION HABIT

Meditation is emerging as a stress management tool which has been rigorously examined by the medical and scientific 'establishments' and pronounced both respectable and highly beneficial. Research[3] has shown that repeated meditation establishes new neural pathways which prevent the accumulation of stress effects, making the technique a natural stress release mechanism.

There are many different forms of meditation. *Transcendental meditation* requires the practitioner (you) to sit quietly and silently repeat a simple word or phrase such as 'Peace' or 'I am peaceful' or 'The bottom line' or whatever else takes your fancy. This works because the repetition stills and calms the mind, but it does take some time to learn how to 'switch off' other thoughts. *Yoga meditation* requires you to focus on observing your breath, and *Guided meditation*, which is perhaps the easiest and most accessible technique, simply involves listening to a *guided meditation journey* on cassette tape. As Lisa Davis says in her book *Journeys Within: A Source Book of Guided Meditations*[4], guided meditations are structured, they have a precise beginning, middle and end, and each meditation is a self-contained experience. Guided meditations require no practice, and the benefits and results are immediate.

Use the next activity as an opportunity to create an action plan for stress management.

ACTIVITY 19

1   Check back to Activity 15 in which you identified the factors which cause stress for you at work. Take a moment to add any additional factors which may be appropriate for you in your current situation.

The factors which are currently causing me stress:

2   Identify at least three things you can do to reduce or eliminate these stress factors.
    1
    2
    3

3   Note down the date on which you plan to start using your chosen tools for stress management, and the date (perhaps three months later) on which you plan to review progress.

Date when I'm going to start taking positive action to manage my stress:

Date when I'm going to review my progress:

4   On or after your chosen review date, note down the progress you have made:

Summary

- People under pressure respond by feeling excited, energized, challenged and as though they are moving forward
- People under stress respond by feeling exhausted, depressed, indecisive and stuck
- When pressure escalates into stress, the body is overloaded with adrenalin and other associated hormones which are supplied by the nervous system as an *automatic* physiological response to perceived danger
- It is necessary to have some way to release these hormones from your system. This can be done by losing your temper (road rage is a good example of this technique!), or by using one or more techniques specifically designed to switch the body from 'All systems go, Alert' status to 'Normal, At rest' status
- Some common physical symptoms of stress include:
    - eating problems and sleep disorders
    - raised blood pressure, palpitations or breathlessness
    - ulcers, migraines, frequent headaches, muscular pain and
    - illnesses related to the immune system (e.g. colds, flu, etc.)
- The factors which are most usually responsible for causing stress at work are:
    - work environment
    - technology
    - job role
    - relationships
    - career development
    - change
- You can effectively manage the stress in your life by developing one or more of the following habits:
    - exercise habit
    - interests habit
    - communication habit
    - 'be good to yourself' habit
    - meditation habit

Notes

1 Paddison, Sara (1995) *The Hidden Power of the Heart*, Planetary Publications.
2 Glass, Dr Lillian (1992) *He Says, She Says*, Piatkus.
3 Gerber, Dr Richard (1988) *Vibrational Medicine*, Bear & Company Publishing, 1988.
4 Davis, Lisa (1995) *Journeys Within; a source book of guided meditations*, Findhorn Press.

Section 4   The time manager

Introduction

Generally, there are two basic approaches to time management. Approach number one involves **hoping that there will be enough time** to do everything. Usually there isn't, and people who adopt this hopeful approach quickly find themselves becoming short of time and very, very stressed.

Approach number two involves **taking control of time**. Those people who tackle time management head-on and take control of the time at their disposal find that they benefit in numerous ways.

The main benefit of taking control of your time is that you will reduce personal anxiety and stress because you will be able to:

- manage your workload (you know what you have to do and you organize your time so that you can do it)
- achieve improved results and make fewer mistakes (you can progress steadily from task to task without panic or confusion)
- see exactly what you are achieving (objectives are reached and noted)

In this section of the Workbook we will be looking at the specific practical steps you can take in order to take control of your time and make it work for you.

Do you have enough time?

Your relationship with time will depend, to a large extent, on the organization for which you work. You may either:

- battle with time, because there is never enough
- be overwhelmed by time, because there is too much; or
- get along OK with time

ACTIVITY 20

1   How would you describe the relationship between the amount of work you
    have to do and the amount of time available in which to do the work?

    Tick one box only

    (a) Generally, I have time on my hands   ❑

    (b) Generally, there is never sufficient time to get through   ❑
         everything which needs my attention

    (c) Although I can't say I always have enough time, the gap   ❑
         between work and time makes me feel challenged and
         stretched. It's OK

2   What do you think is the main reason for your relationship with time being the
    way that it is?

FEEDBACK

The way in which these relationships work are shown in Figure 12 below.

Amount of work you have to get through	Amount of time you have available	How you feel about this relationship
□ →	⬛	**Bored** Undervalued ☹ Not reaching your potential
⬛ →	□	**Panic-stricken** Overworked ☹ Stressed Unable to cope
⬛ →	□	**Challenged** Steadily working ☺ towards achievable objectives

Figure 12   Three kinds of relationships we can have with time and work

Maybe, in response to the previous activity, you were able to say that, generally, you feel challenged by the work/time relationship, but are able to work steadily towards your objectives. This means that your workload is under control. You will be under pressure to some extent – but this will be a level of pressure which motivates you and gives you the confidence to continue to work hard towards achieving your objectives.

If you responded by saying that your current work/time relationship leaves you bored and with time on your hands, then you are likely to be feeling as though time is passing you by and that you are not achieving your full potential.

If, like many managers, you feel that there is too much work and just not enough time, then you will be suffering from stress, and it is time to look at ways in which you can manage your time more effectively.

Planning your time

At work you have four kinds of time-slots. By recognizing and planning for these different time-slots you can make the most of the time available to you, and organize your workload more effectively.

FIXED TIME-SLOTS

These are the parts of the day (week or month) where you know you have regular, fixed activities. For example:

- First Monday of the month, 9.30–12 noon: Marketing meeting
- Thursday of every week, 10.00–12.30: Team meeting
- Friday of every week: 9 a.m.–5.30 p.m.: checking figures, correlating statistics and data, preparing draft report for Finance team

FLEXIBLE TIME-SLOTS

These are the times when you attend to urgent/important tasks as well as routine tasks such as correspondence, phone calls, networking and so on.

PERSONAL TIME-SLOTS

These are blocks of time during which you can work on special projects which will move you closer towards achieving your own **personal work objectives.** Personal time-slots should be blocked out in your diary as 'strictly personal, do-not-disturb' time. Managers who don't recognize the importance of personal time-slots are the people who either don't turn in projects and reports on time, or who do this work at home in the evening or at the weekend **because there isn't enough time during the working week.**

UNEXPECTED TIME-SLOTS

These are those unexpected chunks of time which crop up now and then. You can't plan for them, because they are **unexpected,** but you can prepare in advance so that you can make the most of them, when they occur.

Figure 13 below shows how one manager has set up his diary to allow for fixed time, flexible time and personal time.

Monday 4 November	Tuesday 5 November	Wednesday 6 November	Thursday 7 November	Friday 8 November
8	8	8	8	8 Personal time
9 Team meeting	9 Project planning	9 Flexible time	9 Health & Safety	9
10 Fixed time	10 Fixed time	10	10 Fixed time	10
11	11	11	11 Flexible time	11 Flexible time
12	12 Flexible time	12	12	12
1	1	1	1	1
2 Flexible time	2 Flexible time	2 Flexible time	2 Board meeting	2 Flexible time
3	3	3	3 Fixed time	3
4	4 Personal time	4	4	4
5	5	5	5	5
6	6	6	6	6

Key

These boxes indicate *fixed* time-slots – e.g. regular meetings, etc. which can be entered into the diary in advance

These boxes indicate *personal* time-slots – e.g. times which you can devote to your own tasks and objectives (e.g. writing reports, gathering data, planning campaigns, etc.)

These boxes indicate *flexible* time-slots – e.g. times when you will attend to correspondence, take phone calls, network with colleagues and suppliers, attend one-off meetings, etc.

Figure 13 Diary for week Monday 4 November to Friday 8 November blocked out according to different types of time-slots

One of the keys to effective time management is planning ahead. Obviously you can't do anything about fixed time meetings, and if the Board wants you in Carlisle every Monday morning, and a major account needs you in London every Tuesday morning, and the team needs you in Edinburgh every Wednesday afternoon, then so be it. But if you plan the time **between** fixed time-slots, then you will immediately find that you can manage your workload more effectively.

Use the next activity as an opportunity to experiment with blocking out specific time-slots so that, between fixed time segments, you can plan ahead to give yourself flexible time and personal time.

ACTIVITY 21

Look back through your work diary for the past month or so, and choose a busy week. In the diary sheet below, mark in your *fixed* time-slots. Then divide the remaining time into *flexible* time and *personal* time. Look for ways in which you can save time by grouping similar activities together in the flexible time-slots, and allocate personal time for your own projects.

Monday	Tuesday	Wednesday	Thursday	Friday
8	8	8	8	8
9	9	9	9	9
10	10	10	10	10
11	11	11	11	11
12	12	12	12	12
1	1	1	1	1
2	2	2	2	2
3	3	3	3	3
4	4	4	4	4
5	5	5	5	5
6	6	6	6	6

Naturally, everyone's workload is different, but here are some practical suggestions as to how you can plan your week effectively and use your diary as an important management tool.

FIXED TIME

There isn't a great deal you can do about this. The fixed time-slots are those which, to a large extent, are controlled by other people.

FLEXIBLE TIME

This is the time over which you have a great deal of control. A key technique for managing this kind of time is to 'chunk' similar tasks together. For example, if you specifically dedicate three hours to telephone calls then, during that time, you will make many more calls than if you try to 'slot' them in here and there, during the whole of the week. During your three hours you can work down your list and, if a number is engaged, you just move on to the next call. If people are not available, you can leave a message for them to call you back, and you can move on through your list. Other tasks which can be 'chunked' include:

- mail (reading and writing correspondence)
- reading (reports, proposals, journals, etc.)
- preparing proposals or quotations
- networking with colleagues, suppliers or customers

PERSONAL TIME

This is the type of time-slot which many managers forget to plan. If you have a specific task or project which is your sole responsibility and cannot be delegated, then you really do need to allocate personal time to this.

Rob, a senior manager in retail, explains:

When I moved into management I read all the right books and decided I would keep an open-door policy. It was great for the team because they would pop along at any time and talk through their worries, concerns and problems. But it was a nightmare for me ... every time I settled down to do some of my work there'd be a little tap on the door and my heart would sink.
Within six months I was totally stressed out because I couldn't manage my workload. I was getting into the office before everyone else, staying late and taking work home, just to get some peace. Now I take Monday and Wednesday afternoons as personal time. I shut myself into the office, hold calls, ban visitors and just get on. Obviously, if there's a major, major crisis I'll deal with it ... but otherwise, as far as the team are concerned, I'm out of the building.

The key to success is to be absolutely determined about keeping some part of the working week for yourself – your own work objectives, your own top work priorities. Look at it this way – if you weren't in the office, it would have to wait or someone else would have to deal with it.

UNEXPECTED TIME-SLOTS

Because unexpected time is, by its very nature, unexpected, you can't block it out in your diary. You never know when it's going to crop up. But you can prepare for it so that, when you have a block of unexpected time, you can turn your attention to a meaningful and productive task, rather than wondering 'What'll I do first?' Make a list of the tasks you could usefully do if and when an unexpected time-slot occurs (maybe when a scheduled meeting is cancelled). Use the next activity to create a working list of tasks you can usefully turn your attention to during unexpected time.

ACTIVITY 22

List up to five tasks to which you can give your attention if and when an unexpected time-slot occurs. Clearly, these will not be Urgent and Important tasks, but are the things 'I'd like to get around to when I have the time'.

1
2
3
4
5

The list you created in the previous activity should be regularly updated. As soon as one task is completed and out of the way, add another to the bottom of the list. In this way, if unexpected time is presented to you, it won't be wasted.

Managing your diary

Some key tips for managing your diary:

- Use a pencil, so that when appointments change (as they will) alterations can be made easily and you're not left with pages of messy changes.
- Note down sufficient details, as this will help you to prepare in advance:
  - **2.30 Tom Dawson**, when viewed two weeks later, can cause confusion and even delay if you can't remember the key details
  - **2.30 Tom Dawson, re: Nottingham site – take map and working drawings** is much more helpful and useful

■ Estimate the time you are prepared to spend on each task or meeting and note that down, too. Aim to keep within the time-slots you have allocated for each task or meeting, e.g.:

– **2.30–4p.m. Tom Dawson, re: Nottingham site – take map and working drawings**

Setting a time for completion will allow you to make realistic follow-on appointments and will also enable you to get away from people who want to waste your time (these are the people who are not taking control of **their** time.)

Planning on a daily basis

Careful planning is the cornerstone of good time management, and a 'To Do' list will be of great help to you when planning ahead. To create a working 'To Do' list you need:

■ a master list
■ a daily list

YOUR MASTER LIST

Your master list is a single, continuous list, which is maintained in a notebook. It consists of every single thing you have to do. Throughout each day, every time someone asks you to attend a meeting, find out information, write a report, make a telephone call, whatever – you write down the task on your master list. Every time you think of something which you need to do, write it down on your master list. An example is given in Figure 14 below.

■ Ring Joe about sales figs
■ See Jean re Marshall Bros
■ Arrange doctor's appointment
■ Flowers for Louise
■ 10 p.m. 10 June – meeting with Michael Saunders and Joan Parker re training programme
■ See Sally about chairs

Figure 14   Example of a master list

DAILY 'TO DO' LIST

Either at the **end** of each working day, or the **beginning of the next** working day, you need to take five or ten minutes to transfer items on your master list onto your daily 'To Do' list.

Making your master list work for you

Step 1 Sort out your master list. There will be *Immediate* tasks and *Future* tasks.

Step 2 Transfer the Future tasks into your diary:
- 10 p.m. 10 June – meeting with Michael Saunders and Joan Parker re training programme

Step 3 Transfer the Immediate tasks into your 'daily To Do' list:

To do Wed. 4 September
- Ring Joe about sales figs
- See Jean re Marshall Bros
- Arrange doctor's appointment
- Flowers for Louise
- See Sally about chairs

Step 4 Throughout the day, continue to add to your master list. Tick each task on your daily 'To Do' list as it is completed. At the end of the day, your 'To Do' list might look like this:

To do Wed. 4 September
- Ring Joe about sales figs ✓
- See Jean re Marshall Bros
- Arrange doctor's appointment ✓
- Flowers for Louise ✓
- See Sally about chairs

Step 5 At the end of the day (or the start of the next day), add to your new 'To Do' list the tasks which have not been done. Look at your continuous master list and transfer Immediate items to your 'To Do' list and Future items to your diary:

To do Thurs 5 Sept.
- See Jean re Marshall Bros (from previous 'To Do')
- See Sally about chairs (from previous 'To Do')
- Ring Sam – 0181 339 3681 – re transfer of lease (from master)
- See Lynn re Brian's appraisal (from master)
- Collect air tickets (from master)
- Book car in for a service (from master)

In order to work, your 'To Do' list must be:

- written – 'out of sight, out of mind'. If tasks aren't written down it's easy to forget and lose track of what needs to be done
- updated every single day – **without fail**

PRIORITIZING TASKS

Individual tasks need to be prioritized so that the most urgent and important are attended to first. The techniques of prioritizing using the *Urgent/Important, ABC* and *Paired Comparison* approaches are covered in Workbook 1 of this series, *The Influential Manager*.

Which are your top three time wasters?

Time wasters are those activities:

- in which we consciously become involved
- in which other people involve us

The next activity will give you a chance to think about the three main time wasters which steal your time away.

ACTIVITY 23

List three activities which most often waste time for you at work and then, alongside each time waster you have identified, note down what you have to do to manage the time waster.

1 Time waster:
   How I take control of this time waster:

2 Time waster:
   How I take control of this time waster:

3 Time waster:
   How I take control of this time waster:

FEEDBACK

There are many time wasters which you might have identified, including:

- unexpected visitors to your office
- telephone calls that seem to last forever
- conversations that go round in circles
- meetings that start late, finish late and achieve nothing
- getting drawn into situations you would prefer to avoid (but don't know how to get out of)
- procrastination and indecision

UNEXPECTED VISITORS TO YOUR OFFICE

Having an 'open-door' policy will benefit everyone except you. People, knowing that your door is always open, will pop along to see you **when it suits them**. Once you've committed yourself to an open-door policy it's very difficult to say to people: 'I'm glad you came to see me ... but I'm too busy to talk to you now.' The best way to deal with unexpected visitors is to block out periods of time when you do have an 'open door'. These times might be, say, every morning 8.30–9.30 or Monday, Wednesday and Friday 3.00–5.00 or whenever suits you best. The key to successfully implementing this kind of strategy is to let people know the **days** and **times** when you **are** available. Also, fully brief your secretary so that she can clearly judge whether or not the situation is sufficiently serious to warrant allowing an unexpected visitor to see you. If you don't have a secretary, make a mutually beneficial deal with a colleague. Agree that you will do 'guard duty' for him if he will reciprocate for you. Visitors, when confronted by someone else, will quickly get the message that you really are not available. If there's no other way around it and unexpected visitors do drop in.

- Stand up and don't invite your visitor to sit down
- Greet them politely, but let them know they can have just five minutes
- If it becomes obvious that the reason for the visit is complex and clearly needs more than five minutes, set an appointment when you can get together and give the matter due consideration

TELEPHONE CALLS THAT SEEM TO LAST FOREVER

Before you make a telephone call, note down your objective and your core statement. (Core statements are dealt with in Section 1 of this Workbook; objectives are discussed in detail in Workbook 1: *The Influential Manager*).

Use assertiveness skills to draw the conversation back to the main topic, your objective and your core statement. Don't be afraid to end the call with a simple and courteous statement like, for example, 'Well, you've given me a lot to think about, Harry. It's been really good to talk to you and I'll get back to you within a day or so.'

CONVERSATIONS THAT GO ROUND IN CIRCLES

Again, stick to your objective and your core statement. If it seems as though the conversation is going nowhere, end courteously and assertively. In situations like this, the key point to remember is that even though the other person doesn't mind wasting **his** time, he has no right to waste **your** time.

MEETINGS THAT START LATE, FINISH LATE AND ACHIEVE NOTHING

Lengthy and mismanaged meetings are a tremendous waste of time. There are a number of key steps you can take to ensure that meetings are productive.

■ **If you are attending the meeting:**
  - before you go, make sure you have all the documents you might need
  - confirm with the Chair the date and place of the meeting, and the start and finish times. Make it clear that you have another follow-on appointment and that you will not be available to stay past the anticipated finish time
  - arrive on time
  - acknowledge colleagues and friends, by all means, but be ready to start at the appointed time
  - focus on the items on the agenda and don't waste time by going off at a tangent, or introducing unexpected side issues. You are there to deal with the business in hand
  - listen carefully and contribute your views and opinions
  - at the agreed finishing time gather your papers, remind the Chair that you have another appointment, and leave
■ **If you are chairing the meeting:**
  - start on time
  - keep the discussion focused on the relevant issues
  - encourage people to contribute, ask questions, summarize what has been said or agreed. Prod the group to make a decision. Keep things moving
  - keep a careful eye on the clock and end the meeting on time

GETTING DRAWN INTO SITUATIONS YOU WOULD PREFER TO AVOID (BUT DON'T KNOW HOW TO GET OUT OF)

This happens to everyone from time to time until they learn how to say 'No'.

The key point to remember is that when you say no **you are simply refusing the request, and not rejecting the person**. Every time you agree to do something you know you don't want to do, just think about how much time you will be wasting.

PROCRASTINATION AND INDECISION

We are all familiar with that sinking feeling that comes from looking at a task which involves a great deal of work, and is either complex and difficult, or boring and uninspiring. In these circumstances, it's often tempting to push the task to the bottom of the pile and focus attention on something which is smaller, more interesting, enjoyable and worthwhile. The problem is that the big, complex/boring job doesn't go away. One day, usually when you least feel able to cope with it, it becomes big, complex/boring and very, very urgent. Faced with a task which you really don't want to do, make a commitment to yourself that you will make a start, and then spend some time working on it every day, or even every week. Even a twenty-page report, completed at the rate of two pages per day, will get done in two weeks. Once you start, you might even find that you enjoy it. The key things to remember are:

- Don't put things off because they appear to be 'too big' or 'too difficult'
- Don't always do the easy or the enjoyable tasks first. You'll soon find (surprise, surprise) that there isn't time to do the other stuff
- Plan ahead, prioritize and work to your 'To Do' list

Paperwork

Most managers struggle with a mountain of paperwork, which usually consists of letters, memos, reports, quotations, estimates and/or proposals. The keys to managing paper are:

- Deal with it, or
- Delegate it, or
- Dump it

DEAL WITH IT

Time management experts all agree that the best way to handle incoming paper is to deal with each item only once. So when you look at your daily post you should decide whether to deal with it yourself, delegate it to someone else or dump it.

Many of the documents to which you will need to respond will require a *standard* reply. A good time-saver is to prepare a set of standard letters. For example:

- Thanks for your letter, I'll get back to you (A1)
- Thanks for the invitation, I'll be there (A2)
- Yes, I'd like to (A3)
- No, I don't want to (B1)
- Please pay now (B2)
- Please stop sending me junk mail (B3)

and so on. If your secretary has a set of standard letters, all you need do is to write on each piece of paper (the letter or memo or report you've received) the standard response you would like her to prepare. This will save a great deal of time which can then be devoted to writing or dictating mail which is not standard and which needs an individual approach.

DELEGATE IT

Of course, there will be many items of paperwork which require your personal attention. But do think about which items can be delegated to other people. For instance, if a report arrives on your desk which is not **really** relevant or important but which **might** contain useful information or statistics, pass it on to someone else (your secretary or a junior colleague), tell them the kind of information you want and ask them to read it for you. You can also do this with magazines, journals and newspaper articles.

DUMP IT

Don't be tempted to shuffle papers around or store them in a 'For Later' paper basket. 'Later' never comes. Be ruthless. Ask yourself: 'Can I deal with this?', 'Can I delegate this?', even 'If I never saw this again, would I miss it, and would it matter?'

When looking at ways to improve your time management, do remember Murphy's Ten Laws of Time Management, taken from Patrick Forsyth's book *First Things First*.[1]

1. *If anything can go wrong, it will do so*
2. *Nothing is ever as simple as it seems*
3. *If you mess with something for long enough, it will break*
4. *If you try to please everybody, somebody won't like it*
5. *Nothing ever works out exactly as you expect*
6. *Whatever you want to do, there is always something else you have to do first*
7. *If you explain something so that no-one could possibly misunderstand, someone will*
8. *Nothing is certain until it has happened (and then you should check it more than once)*
9. *If everything goes according to plan, then it is a sure sign that something is about to go wrong*
10. *The only predictable thing about your day is that something totally unexpected will happen*

Use the next activity as an opportunity to create a meaningful action plan to help you take control of your time.

ACTIVITY 24

1a Begin by identifying four practical things you can do to help you take control of your time:

1

2

3

4

1b Note down the date when you intend to put these ideas into action.
Start date:

1c Note down the date when you plan to review progress.
Review date:

2a On the review date (see 1c above), note down your answers to the following questions:

■ What success have you achieved with your time management strategy? What has worked well (i.e. saved time), and what has not worked well?

■ What (if anything) will you do differently in the future?

Summary

■ At work you have four different kinds of time-slots available to you:

■ fixed time-slots (for regular activities such as meetings which occur at specific, fixed times)

■ flexible time-slots (for routine activities such as correspondence, phone calls, meetings, networking and so on)

■ personal time-slots (for working on your own projects, e.g. reports or data collection)

■ Unexpected time-slots (which occur because of cancellations)

- The key to successful time management is:
  - planning ahead and allocating parts of the working week to fixed time, flexible time and personal time activities
  - preparing a list of activities which you can usefully work through when unexpected time presents itself
- Managing your diary by:
  - using a pencil
  - noting details as well as names
  - setting a time limit (start and finish times) will save time
- Your master list is a continuous list of **every single thing** you have to do. Add items to your master list as they crop up
- At the end or beginning of each day, consult your master list and:
  - transfer future items to your diary
  - transfer current items to your 'To Do' list
  - tick each item on your 'To Do' list as soon as it is done
  - at the end or beginning of the day, transfer any items which have not been done to your new 'To Do' list
  - consult your master list and repeat the process
- Prioritize each item on your 'To Do' list and do the most urgent and important things first. Don't do the easy and enjoyable things first
- The three key steps to tackling paperwork are:
  - deal with it, or
  - delegate it, or
  - dump it

Note

1 Forsyth, Patrick (1994) *First things First*, Institute of Management and Pitman Publishing, page 11.

Summary

Now that you have completed the second Workbook in this series, you should feel sufficiently confident to be able to:

- use assertive verbal and non-verbal communication skills
- manage conflict situations
- use a range of stress management techniques
- take control of your time

In Workbook 11, *Getting the Right People to do the Right Job*, we will be focusing on managing human resources, and looking at the skills of effective recruitment, discipline and health and safety.

Topics which have been touched upon in this Workbook are covered in greater depth in other books in this series:

Workbook 1: *The Influential Manager*
Workbook 13: *Building a High Performance Team*
Workbook 16: *Communication*
Workbook 17: *Successful Information Management*

Recommended reading

Davis, Lisa, (1995) *Journeys Within: Source Book of Guided Meditations*, Findhorn Press.

Forsyth, P., (1996) *First Things First*, Institute of Management and Pitman Publishing.

Gerber, Richard, (1988) *Vibrational Medicine*, Bear & Company.

Glass, Dr Lillian, (1992) *He Says, She Says*, Piatkus.

Paddison, Sara, (1992, 1993, 1995) *The Hidden Power of the Heart*, Planetary Publications.

About the Institute of Management

The mission of the Institute of Management (IM) is to promote the development, exercise and recognition of professional management.

The IM is the leading professional organization for managers. Its efforts and resources are devoted to ensuring the continuing development and success of its members.

At the forefront of management standards, the IM provides a range of services for its members. These include flexible training programmes and a unique range of support services such as career counselling, enquiry and research facilities and preferential prices on IM publications and other IM products.

Further details about the Institute of Management may be obtained from:

Institute of Management
Management House
Cottingham Road
Corby
Northants
NN17 1TT

Telephone 01536 204222

We need your views

We really need your views in order to make the Institute of Management Open Learning Programme an even better learning tool for you. Please take time out to complete and return this questionnaire to Tessa Gingell, Pergamon Open Learning, Linacre House, Jordan Hill, Oxford OX2 8DP.

Name:..

Address:...

....

Title of workbook:...

If applicable, please state which qualification you are studying for. If not, please describe what study you are undertaking, and with which organization or college:

....

Please grade the following out of 10 (10 being extremely good, 0 being extremely poor):

Content: ....   Suitability for ability level: ....

Readability: ....   Qualification coverage: ....

What did you particularly like about this workbook?

....

Are there any features you disliked about this workbook? Please identify them.

....

Are there any errors we have missed?
If so, please state page number: ....

How are you using the material? For example, as an open learning course, as a reference resource, as a training resource, etc.

....

How did you hear about the Institue of Management Open Learning Programme?:

Word of mouth: Through my tutor/trainer: Mailshot:

Other (please give details):..

Many thanks for your help in returning this form.

Institute of Management Open Learning Programme

This programme comprises seventeen workbooks, each on a core management topic with the latest management thinking, as well as a *User Guide* and a *Mentor Guide*.

Designed for self study through open learning, the workbooks cover all management experience from team building to budgeting, from the skills of self management to manage strategically for organizational success.

TITLE	ISBN	Price
The Influential Manager	0 7506 3662 9	£22.50
Managing Yourself	0 7506 3661 0	£22.50
Getting the Right People to Do the Right Job	0 7506 3660 2	£22.50
Understanding Business Process Management	0 7506 3659 9	£22.50
Customer Focus	0 7506 3663 7	£22.50
Getting TQM to Work	0 7506 3664 5	£22.50
Leading from the Front	0 7506 3665 3	£22.50
Improving Your Organization's Success	0 7506 3666 1	£22.50
Project Management	0 7506 3667 X	£22.50
Budgeting and Financial Control	0 7506 3668 8	£22.50
Effective Financial and Resource Management	0 7506 3669 6	£22.50
Developing Yourself and Your Staff	0 7506 3670 X	£22.50
Building a High Performance Team	0 7506 3671 8	£22.50
The New Model Leader	0 7506 3672 6	£22.50
Making Rational Decisions	0 7506 3673 4	£22.50
Communication	0 7506 3674 2	£22.50
Successful Information Management	0 7506 3675 0	£22.50
User Guide	0 7506 3676 9	£22.50
Mentor Guide	0 7506 3677 7	£22.50
Full set of workbooks plus *Mentor Guide* and *User Guide*	0 7506 3359 X	£370.00

To order: *(Please quote ISBNs when ordering)*

- College Orders: 01865 314333
- Account holders: 01865 314301
- Individual Purchases: 01865 314627

(Please have credit card details ready)

For further information or to request a full series brochure, please contact:

Tessa Gingell on 01865 314477